Remote Engineering Management

Managing an Engineering Team in a Remote-First World

Alexandra Sunderland

Apress®

Remote Engineering Management: Managing an Engineering Team in a Remote-First World

Alexandra Sunderland
Ottawa, ON, Canada

ISBN-13 (pbk): 978-1-4842-8583-1   ISBN-13 (electronic): 978-1-4842-8584-8
https://doi.org/10.1007/978-1-4842-8584-8

Managing Director, Apress Media LLC: Welmoed Spahr
Acquisitions Editor: Shiva Ramachandran
Development Editor: James Markham
Coordinating Editor: Jessica Vakili

Distributed to the book trade worldwide by Springer Science+Business Media New York, 1 New York Plaza, New York, NY 10004. Phone 1-800-SPRINGER, fax (201) 348-4505, e-mail orders-ny@springer-sbm.com, or visit www.springeronline.com. Apress Media, LLC is a California LLC and the sole member (owner) is Springer Science + Business Media Finance Inc (SSBM Finance Inc). SSBM Finance Inc is a **Delaware** corporation.

For information on translations, please e-mail booktranslations@springernature.com; for reprint, paperback, or audio rights, please e-mail bookpermissions@springernature.com.

Apress titles may be purchased in bulk for academic, corporate, or promotional use. eBook versions and licenses are also available for most titles. For more information, reference our Print and eBook Bulk Sales web page at http://www.apress.com/bulk-sales.

Printed on acid-free paper

To Opa and to Grandma.
I love you both.

Table of Contents

About the Author

Alexandra Sunderland is an engineering leader with over a decade of experience working in both hybrid and remote roles, at companies ranging from ten-person startups to public corporations. She is currently a Senior Engineering Manager at Fellow.app, where she is helping to build the future of work. She prides herself on building emotionally intelligent processes for teams and sharing her knowledge of management through conference talks and written works.

This book is a collection of best practices and lessons that Alexandra has developed throughout her career, meant to help engineering managers new to remote work adapt and become the best leader that they can be—without having to go through the same failures and learnings that she did.

Acknowledgments

To my brother Nicholas, who read through every chapter that I sent his way; thank you for helping me shape this book into something that I'm proud of. Thank you to my parents Deirdre and Jamie, my sister Rebecca, my Oma, and my Grandpa Mark for always cheering me on and always being as excited as I was about this.

Thank you to Anarosa for asking me to be her writing accountability buddy for NaNoWriMo and for the constant encouragement; I wouldn't have ever started writing this if it weren't for her. Thank you also to Laura, Anna, Sarah, and Manuela for always celebrating the highs with me and being there for the lows.

To the entire team at Fellow, who cheered me on throughout this process and always checked in, thank you so much! Everyone asking me how the writing is going meant more than you know. Special thanks to Sam and Aydin who gave valuable feedback on early chapters and made space for me to work on this.

And, of course, thank you to Colin who has always believed in me and has been encouraging me to write a book for the last few years. He kept me caffeinated and on track, gave me the confidence that I didn't always have, and celebrated every little win with me. His constant support means the world.

Introduction

Back in 2012, I got my first ever job as a programmer at a local startup in Ottawa called Fluidware, which built the online survey software FluidSurveys. I was absolutely thrilled, but there was only one problem: I was going to be moving out of town in a few months. I took a chance and asked if I could continue working for the company remotely, something practically unheard of at the time, and to my surprise they said yes! This was back before Slack, Zoom, Google Meet, and all the remote-friendly tools and services that we rely on so heavily nowadays existed. We communicated over Google Chat, phone calls, and email threads.

That early introduction to the world of remote work was just the start. After a while, the company was acquired by SurveyMonkey, where I continued to work remotely and traveled to their international offices from time to time, even working in person full time for a while. In 2018, I rejoined the cofounders of Fluidware who had started a new company, Fellow (a meeting management platform), as the twelfth employee, fifth software engineer, and first remote member. Even though I had worked remotely for companies for seven years already, there was skepticism that being remote would actually work out—and for a while, it was tough. Startups don't have the same resources as large companies, which meant that the meeting rooms didn't have videoconferencing hardware, and everyone had to remember to call me from their laptops so I could join in on discussions. For town hall meetings with the whole company, I was dialled into a laptop which was placed on a chair, as if I were there sitting in the audience with everyone else. It was tricky being the only one, but we made it work.

Fast forward to today, all of Fellow is now operating fully remotely, and we're stronger than ever for it. Being a remote-first company has allowed us to hire across the world, and creates a more level-playing field for everyone: no longer does anyone have to join meetings from a laptop on a chair in a room with poor acoustics! In that time, my role has evolved from Software Engineer to Senior Engineering Manager, where I lead three incredible engineering teams. That growth and the variety of remote experiences that I've had over the years has allowed me to learn a lot about how teams function, and how they differ in operation when working in an office together as opposed to working remotely—with a healthy dash of experimentation to test the boundaries of collaboration.

This book is a collection of the best practices, thoughts, and insights that I have put together throughout the last ten years of working remotely. Many of the concepts I've written about in blog posts and articles, given conference talks on, and created internal guides around within Fellow, but I felt that they deserved to all live together in one single spot that anyone could access. Much of it is based on the many, many mistakes that I've made throughout this whole time. My hope is that other engineering managers who are leading remote teams use this book as a resource that will help them skip over those same mistakes, and lead with a thoughtful and people-first approach.

While the topics themselves aren't specific to remote work, each chapter explains why the remote version is different than the in-person version, and what an engineering manager should do to adapt how they lead to better suit the remote environment. I'll cover topics that aren't often discussed elsewhere, like the remote-specific biases that are introduced when hiring, or why remote one-on-ones are actually *better* than those done in person. Each chapter can stand on its own and be referred back to as needed, but together creates a full picture of how to be a strong remote leader.

And even if your team is not working remotely, or is considering making the switch from remote to office based or hybrid, I hope that you still find the lessons in this book around communication, leadership, and teamwork helpful to your management journey. Because no matter *where* or *how* work happens, teams always deserve to have the best and most thoughtful version of their manager.

CHAPTER 1

Hiring

Before joining your team, every engineer likely experienced the same first few steps: the hiring process. The way that communication with candidates happens and the structure around interviews set the tone for what the work environment will be like, and how they will be treated—far earlier than what might be thought of as someone's first interaction with the company, onboarding.

Setting up an intentionally remote-ready hiring process will help you provide smoother and more positive first experiences for future hires. The best plans make sure that the candidate has a great time interacting with the team, but also put emphasis on the interviewers' experience, by providing proper training and all the necessary information to make them successful. In this chapter, we'll cover the lifecycle of hiring an engineer: from creating remote-first processes to dealing with technology challenges, and to addressing remote-specific biases, there is a lot of planning that goes into making interviews run smoothly. The effort is well worth it, leading to better hiring rates and a more relaxed hiring team.

Every company's hiring process varies, and many teams within the same company also do things a little differently from each other. In most cases, the process will be strung together with the following steps:

1. Job application

2. Screening call with a recruiter/hiring manager

3. Panel interview with future teammates

4. Asynchronous technical test

© Alexandra Sunderland 2022
A. Sunderland, *Remote Engineering Management*,
https://doi.org/10.1007/978-1-4842-8584-8_1

Whether there are multiple of some of the steps or they're set up in a different order, these are each individually common in engineering interview processes. And believe it or not, remote work makes all of these steps better, for everyone—interviewers and candidates alike. We'll step through each one to understand the role remote plays in each, and how the processes may differ from when interviewing someone in person.

The Job Application Form

The first step to any hiring process, whether they're actively applying or are being recruited, involves collecting information from the applicant—at the very least, through a resume.

Even office-based companies will collect applications online so it might seem at first glance that there's no need to differentiate between the two, and for the most part that's correct; there are however some small but powerful bits of information to be added to the job description that make all the difference.

Companies that truly embrace remote work are able to show it through their job descriptions or careers site by providing information such as

- **The geographical areas they can hire from:** One of the great benefits of being a remote company is that you aren't limited in hiring people who live physically close to some central office—you could possibly hire throughout the country, or even the world. For many companies though, hiring is still limited to specific areas due to legal and logistical reasons when hiring in other countries. Specifying the area you're able to hire from starts to narrow down the applications you'll receive.

- **The working time zone:** Different companies (and possibly even different teams within them) will have varying approaches to work schedules. Some companies might truly embrace the "async" lifestyle and allow people to work at whatever time suits them best, but others might require work to happen during a defined period of time—usually typical "work hours" for a given time zone. This doesn't mean that they have to live within that time zone! Some might prefer work hours that fall during their night so they get to enjoy the daytime. Specifying those requirements up front clarifies expectations for applicants before they invest too much time in applying somewhere that won't suit their desired hours.

- **What the company does to foster a strong team culture:** Are there deliberate remote team events set up on a recurring basis? How do people meet others that aren't on their team? Are there fun Slack channels for non-work banter? There are many ways that social connections can be fostered and remote cultures created. Describing some of those initiatives demonstrates that it's something that's actively being thought about, and not being left to chance.

- **Remote-specific benefits:** There are many types of benefits that might be offered to remote employees that you won't typically find otherwise: things like weeklong getaways to a resort every year with the entire company, monthly care packages, office setup stipends, internet cost reimbursement, ... These items all influence the perception of the company and are important to include in the job description.

If you fall into the category of teams that are able to hire remotely outside of your own country, congratulations! Being able to hire without geography as a limitation can lead to more diverse teams, and truly incredible people with vastly different backgrounds. When looking through those applications, it's important to be aware that the culture around resumes and job applications is different around the world. Things like age, marital status, or photos might be on resumes and appear strange (or even illegal) to North Americans, for example, while being common (or even required) in many countries around the world. It's always good to evaluate resumes for just the information that they convey about the person's ability to do the job at hand, but special attention needs to be paid when making decisions on applicants from cultures we're less familiar with to make sure that we aren't unfairly biasing against them for something that's perfectly normal to them.

The Screening Call

Screening calls are either phone calls or video calls that happen early on in the process, and typically last anywhere from 15 to 45 minutes. Depending on how the process is set up, they're hosted by either an in-house recruiter or the hiring manager (you!), and are meant to act as a filter to make sure that there's culture, values, and expectation alignment at a high level before investing too much time on either side. This step is just as much for the company to assess candidates as it is for candidates to assess the company and determine whether it's the right fit for them. Even if you're working out of an office, these screening calls aren't normally done in person because of the small amount of time spent on them: you wouldn't want anyone to invest an hour or two in travel time just for a 15-minute conversation at the very start of the recruitment process.

The key points to cover in the screening calls include

- **Describing the role and team:** This is a good way to start off the call so that everyone is on the same page about what the role is (especially if they've applied to multiple positions at the same company), and go into more depth. It's unlikely that the job posting included information about the makeup or size of the team—talking about this can start to build a connection between the candidate and the role.

- **Describing the company's approach to remote work:** There are many flavors of remote work, and not every company handles things in the same way. Some might be entirely asynchronous based; others require you to be online and available for set hours in the day. Some might organize social events to build bonds across teams, and others might take more of a hands-off approach. "Remote" means so many things; it's worth spending the time to explain what remote is like at your company so that no one joins with expectations of one thing, only to be disappointed.

- **Alignment between their work experience/ aspirations and the requirements for the role:** This is the main portion of the call, where you dive into their past experience, talk about what they're excited to work on, and possibly a situational behavior question or two to make sure that there isn't a complete value mismatch that would prevent them from succeeding in the role. As excited about someone as you might be (or as desperate as you might be), if the candidate is looking for a role without an on-call rotation because they have a newborn, and are hoping to dedicate the next phase of their career to frontend development, don't twist words and try to pass off the machine learning high-alert weeklong-on-call job as if it's a fit. They *will* find out, and they *will* drop out of the process when they do.

- **The salary range being offered:** Ideally just as a repetition of what's already on the job posting! Not only does posting a salary range eliminate the awkward dance of asking someone what their expectations are, it also helps to reduce pay gaps between members of underrepresented groups and their peers brought on by undervaluing oneself or not negotiating (gaps which may be small at first, compound over time, and cause mass disparities later on[1]).

- **Checking for a remote work mindset:** Being a successful remote engineer goes beyond writing great code: strong communication practices and a willingness to participate asynchronously on a team are important factors in how someone will perform. If your team has particular expectations about how work will be done, have a list of questions on hand that can help evaluate whether the applicant will thrive (or even enjoy) working in that way, based on the values you've identified as being the most pertinent to remote work on your team. Some example questions you can use to check for remote readiness are

---

[1] Lara Hogan describes this issue and how to correct it in this article: `https://increment.com/teams/pay-fair/`

- What communication tools do you use, and in what situations do they work best?

- How do you balance work and personal life?

- How do you collaborate with teammates when you're stuck on a problem?

- How do you convey your work's status to your colleagues and manager?

The best screening calls will feel conversational, and the applicants will be asking questions throughout—but that isn't always the case, so it's always important to leave dedicated time for them to ask any questions they may have. If a clear decision has been made in your mind and you're a few minutes short of the meeting's official end time, it's okay to end early! Giving people time back goes hand in hand with the best approaches to remote work.

Panel Interviews

Once the candidate has passed the screening stage and there's deemed to be a mutual fit between both them and the company, they move on to the panel interview stage—also known as the "onsite" in office environments.

This stage can take many forms: it might be an hour of talking with a group of people, six hours in a row of talking with a rotating group, or even more time broken up across multiple days. Some companies are known to book entire days with candidates and have a large panel of various engineers and potential future teammates talk with them, but more often than not, this method is seen as a waste of time (people often make up their minds about whether to move forward with a candidate within the first few minutes of talking).

The panel interview typically involves standard interview questions that lead them to talk through their background and previous experience, their goals, and what they'd like to work on—very similar to the screening call, but in depth, and with subject matter experts. There are often a handful of situational and behavioral questions, and famously in the engineering hiring world, some form of skill testing—usually in the form of a "whiteboarding" question. This is where the interviewers will pose a nontrivial coding question that can take approximately an hour to work through, while guiding them through it. This is a highly controversial step in the process; while many claim (rightfully) that it's important to properly assess someone's coding skills before hiring them, others (also rightfully) argue that we rarely code under pressure with teammates overlooking us, judging every semicolon (or lack thereof). Alternative skill-testing tasks are becoming more and more popular; reviewing pull requests, completing small take-home projects, or doing real-time non-algorithmic code challenges are often preferred to whiteboarding interviews. These newer styles of interviews give a better look into how someone will actually perform on the job, and when structured well, don't require a particular type of educational background to excel in. There are many stories and arguments both in favor and against the whiteboarding type of interview, but whatever your company's practice is, there is setup and preparation that will need to be done to make this effective remotely.

For in-person positions, interviews can take up an incredible amount of time from everyone involved. The candidate needs to physically travel to the office (likely dealing with public transit or parking situations), plan to arrive early enough to sign in and get a tour, and then spend hours sitting in a room talking to a rotating set of people, before travelling all the way back home. Worst of all, because they've made the commitment to get all the way to the office, even if it's determined really early on in the interview that it's in everyone's best interest not to continue with the process (perhaps because of a deep skillset mismatch or misunderstanding of the role), people will be "kind" and continue through the whole process for the time that they've been booked to be there, so as to not appear rude or upset them.

In remote panel interviews, everyone has a big advantage: since no one has had to invest a lot of time in travel to get to the interview, it's far easier to get over the mental and emotional hurdle of ending early if needed. I would never recommend talking to someone for less than five minutes before making the call to end it unless something is terribly wrong, but if you have a two-hour interview scheduled and it's clear within twenty minutes that there's a mismatch and they will not be successful, it isn't rude to cancel the rest of the interview. And they won't hate you for it! They may be disappointed, but overall they will likely be glad that all of that extra time wasn't wasted for nothing, and it lets them get out of a stressful situation more quickly. Ending an interview early should be reserved for rare and objective cases though, and not for just mediocre performance with one interviewer: people will act differently with a range of interviewers because of how personalities mesh, and it's only fair to give them the chance to talk to the whole panel. When telling the applicant that you'll be ending early (and it's clearly much earlier than the scheduled end time), let them know directly why: whether it's the too-large gap in expected skills, the values mismatch, or whatever it may be, the feedback in the moment will avoid leaving them wondering what went wrong.

Tip   When briefing the panelists on the interview structure, set up a plan of action for what to do if an interview shouldn't be continued. Let them know if/when they have the right to make that decision, how to notify the other subsequent panelists that it's over, and how to communicate it to the applicant.

In most cases though, hopefully everything is going well! During your interview, you'll want to make sure to be taking notes about the candidate so that you don't forget any important details or thoughts. When you are interviewing many people within a short timeframe, it can be difficult to properly remember how each interview went; to avoid creating an unfair advantage to the people that you spoke with the most recently, the details of each conversation should be written down so it's easier to jog your memory after the fact when reviewing all the candidates. Consider muting your microphone or using software to cancel out the noise of your keyboard while you're typing to avoid causing a distraction—or stressing out the candidate who will be wondering what they could have said that made you want to start writing things down!

If you have your camera on and the candidate can see you on the call, or if you have your microphone enabled and the sound of your keyboard comes through it, the person will likely notice you looking off to the side or hear the sound of the keys tapping and wonder who you're Slacking or why you're emailing people when you're supposed to be listening to them. They probably can't see your screen and won't know what you're doing, so make sure to let them know right at the start of the call that if you're looking off to the side or typing, you're taking notes so that you don't forget any important details—not ignoring them. They will appreciate the heads-up, and it will also signal to them that you care about what they're saying and are invested in the process. Don't spend the entire time taking notes though: not every little detail needs to be written down; save the typing for the important points that you don't want to forget, and overall impressions. If the panels are set up so that multiple people are interviewing the person at the same time, either designate one person as the note taker or take turns so that when one person asks a question, the other takes notes: this will make it feel like more focus is being given to the applicant.

When you aren't taking notes, make sure that they can see that they have your full focus and attention. If your camera is on, look right ahead into the camera and nod your head and smile when they're talking—this will both show that you're engaged in the conversation and be a good indication that you're still on the call and that no, your internet hasn't frozen (it might look that way if you sit there without moving for a while). Try to avoid making too many noises; while affirming "mhmm" sounds can be comforting in person and make it clear that you're actively listening and engaged with what's being said, it doesn't carry that way over a call. Even the most subtle of lags can delay the sound enough that it comes across as though you're constantly interrupting them and trying to get them to hurry up—which can be quite flustering, trip up the applicant, and make speaking awkward. This can also be a difficult habit to break, in which case going on mute while they're speaking works in a pinch!

If your interview process includes some form of collaboration, whether it's a coding test or a whiteboard-style free-form drawing "Systems Design" interview, you're going to need to leverage some technology—unless you're resorting to drawing back and forth on paper and holding it up to the camera (not a great first solution, but it's an option when all else fails). There are many collaboration tools that exist for this purpose. You'll want to make sure you know what tool you're using well ahead of time, so that when the interview is scheduled, the emailed invitation can include a link to the tool that will be used, information on how it will be used, and even possibly a tutorial highlighting the main elements that will be used. The goal here is to reduce the number of surprises that the candidate will encounter in an interview so that they can be as successful as possible. Most people will have used a physical whiteboard before, and the barrier to entry in terms of knowledge to use one is quite low in case they haven't. But when it comes to technology, we're all used to specific tools, and it may cause a tad of panic if we need to figure out on the spot (in front of people!) how to use the specific tool that they want, all while trying to start thinking of a solution to the tough problem being presented—with a potential job on the line. Plus, not everyone is joining interviews from a large home office setup with large secondary monitors at the ready and lots of screen real estate. A warning ahead of time that a tab other than the video call will need to be opened gives them the opportunity to arrange their windows to best suit that need. A quick note about the tool picked: unless you have a very good reason, try to avoid using a tool that will require them to sign up for an account to join the interview. This is an extra barrier that may use up time during the interview!

Tip   Always have a backup plan in case the usual tool being used for the technical test isn't an option during an interview (whether there's an outage, it's blocked in the applicant's country, isn't compatible with any assistive technology they use, or whatever the reason may be). Even if it means switching to Google Docs for coding, that's better than rescheduling or cancelling the interview.

Asynchronous Technical Test

The next common step in an engineering hiring process is the asynchronous technical test.

There are many variations to this, and some processes might even include multiple types of tests scattered throughout—for example, a sub-one-hour basic programming challenge where written code is run against automated tests as a screening phase before speaking to a recruiter, or a longer-form project with more space for creativity near the end of the process which is evaluated by actual engineers on the team.

Whatever the test actually contains, it's done by the candidates on their own time and not in front of anyone on the hiring panel (like we talked about in the last section). Being done on their own time makes it an asynchronous step, because they will be sent the task to complete at some point, submit it when they're ready, and the hiring panel will review it (also when they are ready). If you're using a system like HackerRank to send out automatically graded code challenges, this step becomes fairly simple for the interviewer since everything from the sending to the scoring can be set up to be automatic—though I recommend including a dash of manual effort to review tests, especially low-scoring ones which may have failed test cases on a technicality and have otherwise solid solutions. But if you're sending off a larger project along the lines of instructing them to build something according to some specification, or even add new features onto some prebuilt app you provide, there's a lot more room for error and for unfair technological issues to pop up, and it's worth investing a tad more effort into creating proper communication channels so that the candidate can be set up for success.

But first, on the technical test itself. Take-home projects in interviews are a controversial topic! Some engineers love them for the chance to demonstrate how they're able to write code, possibly as a substitute to live coding in front of interviewers, which can be an anxiety-inducing task that leads to poor performance and the loss of a job opportunity. Others feel that companies should provide compensation to candidates for their time spent on these projects (regardless of the actual work product) because they can require spending a significant amount of time to finish, which can feel unfair and like unpaid labor. However you feel about the tests themselves and their particular usefulness in making a hiring decision, there is a reality to them that needs to be taken into account if they are a part of your process: the length of time that candidates will need to dedicate to them. A typical take-home coding challenge should take no more than two to three hours of someone's time, with eight hours being an absolute maximum. There are many reasons for this:

- They are likely interviewing at multiple companies, and all these tests add up to a lot of time overall. If your test is too long, they may decide that it isn't worth their effort to do, and will drop out of the interview process.

- If the test is too long, they might not have time to work on it during the week, and might schedule to complete it over the weekend. Assuming your company operates on a typical Monday-Friday workweek, that's extending your hiring lead time by up to seven days, during which time they're talking to other companies and continuing to move through those pipelines.

- It makes it look like you don't value their time as humans. If you're asking someone who doesn't even work there yet to dedicate a large number of hours to this task, what will you make them do once they've signed on to the team?

- It makes the team appear to be disorganized. What could be learned from a 24+ hour test that couldn't be learned from a shorter one? Why has it been structured in that way?

But the most important reason: the type of person that can dedicate many hours of their life to completing a timed code test on short notice is a very particular type of person. It's likely someone without kids or dependents, and without nonnegotiable obligations outside of work that take up their time (maybe working a second job, doing volunteer work, or undergoing routine medical treatment). By asking someone to complete a multi-hour assignment for free, the number of people who will be successful in your process is being artificially limited, and it's creating a more homogenous group of people who reach the end of the pipeline. This is not good for the overall diversity and makeup of the team (or the people in the industry itself), and so it's best to limit the length of this test to two to three hours if you do have one—the same amount of time that you would expect them to dedicate to a panel interview.

Timing aside, there is work around creating the right atmosphere for asynchronous communication during the technical challenge too. If you're setting up a take-home test that involves candidates running code locally on their own computer (and not in some click-to-load virtual environment on the Web), creating a space to communicate around tech issues is a great way to show that you want the candidate to be successful, you care about them, and that the team is a supportive one.

On the engineering teams at Fellow when we've scheduled the take-home challenge with an applicant, we create a private Slack channel with the hiring panel, and invite the candidate as a guest user (which gives them access to join that single channel in the workspace for free). We send off the invitation to join this as soon as possible. It gives people a space to say hi and make connections with the engineers on the team if they're so inclined, but there's no pressure to do so, and it doesn't factor into our final decision either way. When they're getting their technical test set up, we make it very clear that we want them to be as successful as possible, and that if there are any issues (such as invalid environments on their computer, or Python version mismatches) that they can't solve on their own, we will gladly help out. We've gone through great lengths to make the test as simple as possible to get set up on any computer and to make sure that it goes smoothly, so this isn't something that people normally take advantage of. However, it's a great safety net to make them feel more confident and less worried about something out of their control happening, which means that they perform better overall too. We deactivate this channel 24 hours after we've gone over the code with them, so that it doesn't feel as though we're "done with them" if we were to close it down immediately.

The idea behind this asynchronous Slack channel is adapted from an idea that Katie Wilde, former VP of Engineering at Buffer, brought up on the Supermanagers podcast.[2] At Buffer, these Slack channels are created so that the hiring panel and candidate can ask each other actual long-form interview questions and write back answers asynchronously (with reasonable expectations on receiving answers within approximately 24 hours on business days). Not only does this make the interview potentially less stressful for candidates by not putting them on the spot and respecting that they have other responsibilities going on in life to get to, it also shows their skills in communicating in written format—a set of skills that are incredibly important for someone who is going to be joining a fully remote team.

After someone invests all of this time into their test, they should be provided with feedback on how they did—regardless of whether they are moving forward into the next stage in the process. It's demoralizing to receive a rejection from a company in the first place, but can be even more so when you've put so much time and effort into writing code for one and receive nothing more than an email informing you that you didn't quite make the cut, without explaining why. There will likely be comparatively few people making it to this stage in the interview process, and sending just a few sentences explaining for every person that is not moving forward will be the world of a difference in how they'll feel about their interview experience.

How to Schedule Interviews

When it comes to scheduling screening calls, ditch any and all efforts at manually trying to coordinate a time to talk.

---

[2] https://fellow.app/supermanagers/katie-wilde-buffer-4-steps-to-remote-success/

It. Will. Not. Work.

The back and forth of "What time works best for you?" might be enough when trying to plan a coffee date with friends, but ends in disaster when trying to plan something as simple as a call between two busy people during work hours, with constantly changing availability. The three time slots you pitch to an applicant might quickly be scooped up by the other ten people that got back to you first, and the email chain will be a dozen messages deep before one of you gives up and halts the interview process altogether. Or worse, you do manage to find a time where you're both free, but the time zone wasn't specified and now the applicant is anxiously waiting by the phone at 2pm in EST, while you're blissfully unaware at 11am PST, getting ready for your 2pm PST call.

Instead of going through this scheduling nightmare, use a tool like Calendly, which integrates directly with your calendar and allows specifying availability time slots so that anyone with the link can book meetings with you directly. This fixes multiple issues:

- The options will be displayed in the viewer's time zone, so there's no confusion about what time the event is really scheduled for.

- They will see every possible time slot (with real-time availability) which reduces stress from needing to suggest their own times, and eliminates many back and forth emails (shortening the time from first contact to interview too, and reducing your own cognitive load).

- Event rescheduling and cancelling is built-in and handled through the same interface, removing the need to manage the calendar manually altogether.

It's overall a win-win for everyone, and frees up a lot of time on all sides. This scheduling strategy also applies to other types of interviews, which can be even more complicated since they're being scheduled on behalf of a group of engineers. Calendly even includes group booking functionality, where everyone's availability is taken into account when displaying available time slots.

What to Do When Technology Fails

Because let's face it, *it will*.

When we're on calls during meetings with colleagues and our internet cuts out, we might even think…yay! It's like a snow day—school's out, and you have this time blocked on your calendar without needing to do that thing it's blocked for. When the internet cuts out during an interview, it's a whole other story. No matter whose side it's on, the interviewee will be nervous and worried about what it means for them and their job prospect. It's up to you, the interviewer, to find a solution and get things back on track as quickly as possible. Here's a rundown of what you can do:

1. If the internet is still up and someone is just frozen on the screen, use the chat functionality if available to make them aware of the situation.

2. If the audio/video is choppy, everyone on the call should turn off their video so that the amount of data being transmitted is lower and the audio has a higher chance of making it through properly.

3. If nothing's coming through, send them a quick email with options. If your meeting scheduling service provides alternative methods to join the call, such as a phone number, suggest using that to finish off the conversation and join it while you wait for a response. This is a big benefit of using Google Calendar for events, which provides both a Google Meet URL and a phone number to join the same call.

4. In the situation where the interview cannot continue
   (the internet is completely down, something
   happened in person on either end such as a fire
   alarm sounding, ...), let the rest of the interview
   panel know, and send the candidate an email with
   options to reschedule the call. Tech issues are no
   one's fault, and they shouldn't get in the way of
   determining whether someone should join the
   team. If the interview was coming to an end anyway,
   this portion can be skipped, but do let them know
   what the status is and thank them for their time, as
   you would do at the end of the call.

And lastly, if you have a strict interview process with very specific time limits for different portions, building in some buffer time for any eventual (and definite) tech issues that come up—or washroom breaks—can prevent each section from running over time and getting off track.

A New Set of Biases

When you're interviewing a candidate, there are all sorts of biases that are important to be aware of and to try to minimize as much as possible.

We all have biases, and as long as we're aware of them and do our best to adjust for them, we can work toward creating a more fair and just process overall. Some common biases include feeling that people with a heavy foreign accent are less competent than those who speak the working language with a native accent, believing that older candidates will be less invested in the job than those who are younger, or preferring to hire people from particular schools which are known to incur high tuition costs and are located in affluent areas (therefore typically hosting people from a particular type of upbringing). There are some ways to mitigate the effect of these biases, such as having a hiring panel made up of a diverse group of people representing as many backgrounds as possible. The general topic goes far beyond what can be reasonably covered in this book outside of the remote-specific aspects, but is incredibly important for any engineering team, the people on that team, and the community at large. The time and energy put into researching biases in hiring and implementing real changes is well worth it.

When interviewing remotely, there is an entirely new set of potential biases to be aware of, which are based off of far less apparent (or possibly, even undetectable) aspects of people's own situations, compared to when interviewing in person in an office.

Bias #1: Internet Quality

The first potential bias-inducing aspect of a remote interview is the candidate's audio, video, or overall internet quality during the calls.

When the audio-visual quality over a call is low, including lag, choppy voices, or a pixelated face, those speaking might appear less competent than others coming across more clearly, because it's easier to process the information that they're conveying. Given two equally strong candidates, the one with the clearer picture could very well be viewed more favorably because they were easier to understand and communicate with, through no fault of their own. There are many reasons why someone's home setup might not be ideal for the interview call: most notably, it's expensive! There's a reason that "Work from Home" stipends are commonly offered. If they aren't already working for a remote company that has provided them with a good desk and technology setup (or they haven't yet picked up podcasting as a hobby), it's unlikely that they will have spent a lot of their own money on equipment just for calls. As for the internet, they may not even have a choice.

When hiring remotely, you're not limited to candidates that live close to any particular office, and it's highly likely that you'll end up interviewing someone who lives in a rural area—and in countries like Canada and the

USA, rural areas aren't serviced for the internet as equally as the larger cities are. A large portion of both countries still rely on dial-up internet connections for lack of better options, and even in its largest cities, internet costs in Canada are among the highest in the world.

To judge someone's competence based on the quality of how they're coming across on the screen, even unknowingly, is unfair. If the quality is causing issues in communication (constantly freezing, voice not quite making it through, ...), these issues are easy to fix after the candidate has been hired: the company can send equipment over, and potentially subsidize the cost of their home internet connection. In the meantime, speaking over the phone may be a better and more equitable option.

Bias #2: Video Call Backgrounds

The next bias to be on the lookout for is based on their backgrounds.

If you're conducting interviews with cameras on, you'll likely get a glimpse into the person's home life. Many videoconferencing platforms have options to blur your background or choose a custom image to display (and I would highly suggest considering the need for that when choosing a platform for video calls). But those options aren't always on the table, especially in the case where their equipment isn't from the latest and greatest tier. The amount of processing required for blurring backgrounds can be so inhibitive on some machines that the quality of the call would suffer so much that they would fall into the first bias case that we talked about.

So, people may choose not to hide their backgrounds—nor should they need to. The backgrounds that appear on these calls can cause interviewers to form certain impressions about who they are as people, and it's important to avoid doing that as much as possible. It's not likely that the candidates will have a dedicated office space to work out of with a perfectly curated backdrop for their calls. It's much more likely that they're joining the call from the couch, or their kitchen table. In their backgrounds, you might see a messy bed, dishes scattered, unfolded laundry, ... The horror, signs of a normal life! While the first gut reaction is to think that it's unprofessional to show such a messy and not-put-together side to oneself when you're interviewing for a job, it's impossible to understand the circumstances in someone's life that lead to their background being the way that it is. Also, *it's none of your business.* All the information available during that call that can introduce bias is not present when people are interviewing for jobs onsite. It's not even being judged in other ways, it's just not there, there's no home inspection or way of determining whether someone made their bed that morning, and it shouldn't matter. It has no effect on their day-to-day job as an engineer. This leads us into our next bias: distractions.

Bias #3: Noise

When we're working remotely, there are certain benefits that come inherently with that. We're home when we're waiting for a package, and we won't miss the delivery or have it sitting outside all day. If we have kids, we can hang out with them throughout the day, eat meals together, and watch them grow up. It can be great! But the world doesn't stop around us when we join a call, and it doesn't for the people that are being interviewed either.

Interviews are one of those higher-stakes type of meetings where impressions really matter and everyone knows it. It's not quite like meeting with your close-knit team where you can run off for a quick second when the doorbell rings, or bring your cat up to say hello, without worrying about whether you'll be looked down upon or seen as unprofessional (at least, I hope that you have a team where these things are okay). While we can try to minimize distractions as much as possible, sometimes they're just inevitable. And not all distractions are created equally! Take sound-based distraction for example. If someone has a dog bark in the background in their home, it may even reflect positively on them subconsciously (dogs require time, effort, and money to take care of, and if someone has one, it could possibly be a sign that they are in a good place financially). But if there's someone who yells outside their home, it could have the opposite effect, and we might end up having an inferior opinion of them overall compared to other candidates, regardless of how they actually performed in the interview itself. The same goes for distractions from kids: it's well known that women of childbearing age in the workplace are at a disadvantage because of the bias of assuming that they will be leaving or taking time off to raise a family, and that men do not suffer from that same assumption (they actually progress because of it). If a child causes a distraction during an interview with a man, he may be looked upon favorably as a family man, while that same distraction will make a nonmale candidate be looked down upon because of the assumption that their childcare duties may have a higher priority, and that their work will not be accomplished. Those biases that are more common in day-to-day life start to creep into the remote world of work, and we have to explicitly be on the lookout for them and make sure that we're doing our best to not be affected by them.

Winning People Over When They Have Multiple Offers

Earlier in this chapter, we talked about how one of the benefits of hiring remotely is that the talent pool is a lot wider than it is for those hiring out of an office setting. The same is true for engineers: they can choose to work for far more companies when they aren't limited by physical proximity, and can end up with offers from companies all over the country by the time they're done with their interview rounds.

It's very likely that when you make someone an offer, you'll be competing against startups, mid-size companies, and large companies alike. At this stage, there's not a lot you can do to change the company itself to attract them (the benefits are what they are, and you can't usually create their dream project out of thin air). But there are a few things you can do to win them over! One of the main differentiators between companies is the team culture: compensation is extremely important, but no one wants to join a team that doesn't get along, and given similar monetary incentives, the company with the better culture will be chosen.

When making engineers offers to join the company, I'll have already spent a long time pitching them on the team and company culture in the interview process, but after the offer is sent, I'll send over another email explaining why exactly I want *them* on my team. This isn't a cookie-cutter template I automatically send out to everyone, this is a thoughtfully crafted explanation of why we chose them out of the many other people that we talked to over the weeks. In that email, I'll also include information about the team members they'd be working with, outside of those that they'd have already met on the hiring panel. By including links to the team members' professional internet profiles, they're building emotional ties to the team already and can start to envision what their life would be like here. And lastly, to seal the deal, we send gifts! My favorite gift to send is donuts from a bakery, local to the person. I'm normally able to find one that delivers within 24 hours, so it's faster than ordering any other sort of physical gift from an online store. And it feels so personal, because doing that research takes time and effort: there's no central HR system set up that can automatically send out donuts to future hires (yet). That effort and the small cost (maybe $50) goes such a long way toward showing people that we're a human-first team and that we truly care about the people that we work with. It sets a great starting tone for the working relationship. And so far, it's worked every time.

Takeaways from This Chapter

- Before starting to hire, make sure that you understand your company's strategy: are you hiring remote within the city or country, remote anywhere within the same time zone, or anywhere in the world?

- Don't be afraid to end an interview early if it's clear that there's no mutual fit, but prepare the interviewers with the conditions under which this is acceptable to do, and the messaging around it.

- Let the candidate know that you're taking notes so that they don't mistake you typing and looking away for messaging people.

- Use a scheduling tool like Calendly to book interviews and avoid the awful back and forth of emails suggesting times to meet, and instead let candidates see your availability and schedule interviews at their own convenience.

- If you're using extra technology during the interview, give the candidate a heads-up over email at least 24 hours before so that they can get familiar with it and plan out their computer setup.

- Limit take-home technical tests to two to three hours to be cognizant of the candidate's time and to create a more fair and equitable environment for people with obligations outside of work hours. This will also keep the hiring timeline tight because people won't need to schedule take-homes for weekends, which could potentially increase the time between stages by up to seven days.

- To make the candidate feel more confident and to show that you have their best interest and success at heart, create a Slack channel with them as a guest where they can ask any questions around technical issues that they run into during the asynchronous technical test. This is also a great opportunity to see how they communicate remotely, an important and valuable skill for a remote team member.

- Always have a backup plan for what to do when technology fails, whether it's rescheduling the interview, joining via phone call, or using a different meeting service.

- Be highly aware of all the new types of possible biases that are introduced through remote work which aren't present in typical in-person interviews. In particular, avoid making judgments about a candidate's suitableness for the job based on their audio/visual/internet quality, their video background, and any sources of distractions that may arise during the interview.

CHAPTER 2

Onboarding

Back when I started my very first job as a software engineer, I had no idea what I was doing.

I had just turned 17 when I landed a position over the summer at a small self-funded local startup where I'd be building internal tools for the sales and marketing teams. I was using languages I didn't know (JavaScript and Python) to build web applications, whereas I had come from a comfortable background of Java and Visual Basic where UIs were built via drag-n-drop. I didn't know the first thing about building for the Web; I'd never come across servers or HTTP requests, let alone had to build systems to process incoming webhooks and build message queues. To this day, I still clearly remember telling someone that I needed some sort of server to receive webhooks, being handed a post-it note with login credentials to my new server without another word, and then spending all night researching "How to log in to a server" before giving up the next day and asking what on *earth* I was supposed to do with that note.

That summer I spent many nights researching the vast amounts of things that I didn't know so that I wouldn't look silly, sitting at my desk working up the courage to ask someone for help (I didn't know who I was supposed to go to), and being terrified that I wouldn't make it as a programmer because I couldn't type at the speed of light like one of the other developers could (I now know he was abnormally fast, and that isn't a necessary trait to be a programmer). It was an incredible learning

© Alexandra Sunderland 2022
A. Sunderland, *Remote Engineering Management*,
https://doi.org/10.1007/978-1-4842-8584-8_2

experience, but that sort of struggle of being in the unknown can make people really uncomfortable. It's a situation that I've set out to make sure that no one on my team ever has to experience.

Starting a new job is hard, especially when you aren't surrounded by desks filled with people who have all the answers. While with an in-person setup you can *almost* get away with hiring someone and not providing them with a proper onboarding experience because of the support that they'll get from those physically around them, that's not an option for people joining teams remotely. Systems need to be deliberately put in place to properly support new hires and guide them through the start of their new job, to avoid situations like the one that I was in.

It's likely that you're working somewhere where the administrative side of onboarding is already managed by a combination of HR and IT personnel. They might have tasks such as making sure that various forms are signed, email accounts are created, and the necessary payroll information has been provided—maybe even also setting up an employee's first "Welcome Call" with the company for their first day. We'll assume that all of these non-job-specific steps are being managed already, and focus specifically on how to integrate someone into your engineering team. Even if the engineering department already has a dedicated process for onboarding (that's terrific!), it's not enough on its own, and there should still be steps specific to the new person so that they feel welcomed by their particular team.

When I was a Software Engineer at SurveyMonkey, there was an engineering-wide onboarding process that everyone had to follow: new hires would all attend a series of classes in their first week to attain a baseline of knowledge in certain languages and frameworks, before splitting off and working on the teams they were hired into. While the idea was filled with good intentions of levelling the playing field and creating space for people to learn on the job instead of spending time on it outside of work hours, there were a few problems with this. Namely, the classes taught were technology focused, and not every team used the same tech stack. I was the instructor for the "Intro to Jinja Templating" session which was relevant to only a small portion of the people that had to sit through the class, and attendance was required whether you were right out of school or an industry veteran. It wasn't terrific for the engineers who had to sit through my slides demonstrating basic syntax for conditional statements and imports, and it wasn't great for me as an instructor either because I could see how bored everyone was. No matter how hard you try, it's pretty difficult to make a 45-minute-long presentation about the basics of a templating language interesting. If you're implementing an onboarding program from the ground up, I would avoid venturing too soon into these types of classes. While some large companies have created great courses and programs for new hires, they're some of the highest-effort and lowest-impact ways of going about onboarding.

The first-week experience sets the tone for how someone will feel about their team. If the atmosphere isn't particularly welcoming, or existing members don't go out of their way to say hi and show them the ropes, it won't matter how cool the technology they're working on is: they're going to feel like the team doesn't care about their presence, and that will impact their interactions negatively. It can take a long time and a significant amount of effort to undo that kind of impression once it's been left. Creating a great introductory week for them in the first place will help to avoid that whole situation, and start everyone off on the right foot.

To get started with setting up a great onboarding process, you need to be communicating with them early and not just wait until their start date— you need to start the communication at least one week earlier, and ideally as a continuation from the day that they sign their offer letter. The time spent between that day and their start date is a delicate time, where they'll be likely hearing back from other companies they were interviewing with, getting counteroffers from their current employer to convince them to stay, and starting to feel nervous about the process of quitting and starting somewhere brand-new. You want to continue the line of communication with them so that they stay invested in the process and feel more comfortable with their choice, and lower the chances of them reneging on their offer.

The Week Before

No matter how long you've been around in the industry and how many new starts you've had, your first day at a company is always intimidating. It's like the first day of school: you don't know what your day will look like, who your homeroom teacher will be, what the other kids will be like, and most of all—whether or not you'll fit in.

More often than not, when you're joining a new job you're more nervous about the people and the team than the technology. You can't stay up all night cramming to learn how to best work with your new teammates like you can to learn the code. There's also that sense of unpredictability that's creeping up, because they're about to enter a new phase where they have to create new routines and relationships after being able to follow the same known patterns for a while at their previous job. It's a lot to emotionally take on at once!

Welcome Email

To help appease the anxiety that comes with joining a new team, I send out an email at least one week before the new hire's start date with an outline of exactly what to expect in those first few days. It covers everything from what time we're officially kicking off the day (including time zone) to where to go (remotely: the video call link to join), to what their schedule will look like, and even what—if anything—they need to prepare for each meeting they're invited to that week. Having this information available to them ahead of time reduces the amount of uncertainty they'll have about their first week, putting them a little more at ease. This introductory email is also useful for making sure that the start time you've outlined actually works for them: they may have caregiver duties or other obligations in place that need to be worked around, and that start time might be less than ideal.

SAMPLE ONBOARDING EMAIL

Hi Sam,

We're so excited to welcome you to the team! In advance of your start date, we wanted to make sure that you have all the information you'll need about what to expect in the first week. We'll be focusing mostly on getting your development environment set up, familiarizing you with our tools and processes, but most importantly, meeting the team and making connections with others! The schedule for what to expect at a high level is below. Please let me know if you have any personal time conflicts that we should work around, and of course feel free to reach out at any point with questions!

Monday

- We'll start the day with a 10am ET video call to say hi.

- Team check-ins are at 10:30am ET, where you'll get to meet the rest of your team! No need to prepare anything other than an introduction for yourself.

- Today's focus will be getting accounts set up. We'll have a Slack channel dedicated for you to ask your manager and onboarding buddy questions.

Tuesday

- At 2pm ET, we have our weekly engineering team meeting, where you'll get to see demos of in-progress work and tech talks. No need to prepare anything this week!

- ...

...the rest of the schedule for the week...
See you soon,

Alexandra

Onboarding Buddies

As a manager, you're in a position of authority over your team members. As much as you may or may not try to downplay it, that authority has an impact on how people will interact with you—especially when you're just getting to know each other. When remote, that impact is magnified because the majority of interactions you'll likely have are meetings with a purpose, with typically less room for casual conversation than you'd have in an office together. This can translate into team members being more reserved with the questions they ask and less likely to seek out the context that they need to properly understand their work, out of fear that they won't appear knowledgeable or self-sufficient to their new manager. That's not good! While you and your new report are building up your relationship over time and getting to that point where they can ask anything that's on their mind, it's in their (and the company's) best interest to make someone available to them where that reporting structure (and related power dynamic) doesn't hinder learning. That person is the onboarding buddy.

The role of the onboarding buddy is mostly a social one, and can include responsibilities such as

- Being on the first-day call to enthusiastically welcome the new team member

- Checking in throughout the first few weeks to see how the new hire is doing

- Introducing them to other people in the company outside of their direct team, and setting up social time

- Guiding them through the development environment setup process, and walking them through how the project code is structured

- Picking out the first few code tasks for them to work on

- Making themselves available to answer any and all questions about the company, no matter how small or silly the question may seem

- Taking note of and fixing issues, roadblocks, or misunderstandings during onboarding so that the process is even more smooth next time

They handle a lot! So who should you choose for the role? The best onboarding buddies are peers on the same team as the new hire since they'll have the best understanding of the role, and ideally ones that joined the team recently and can better empathize and understand the struggles. The person should also have the time and willingness to participate in the process: onboarding requires a lot of time and energy, and major unmovable deadlines can impede on someone's ability to dedicate the amount of attention required. People who have expressed interest in taking on more mentorship roles could also be the perfect fit for the role! Onboarding buddies should be enthusiastic participants in the process for it to go well and give the new hire the best impression of their new team, so always have a discussion a few weeks before appointing them and lay out the responsibilities and expectations so there are no surprises.

One of the largest responsibilities that the onboarding buddy takes on is that of the question-answerer. The questions that new hires ask aren't just helpful for their own learning—they also provide valuable information for the rest of the team, as they get to see how newcomers perceive how the team operates without. Often, thinking about the questions that get asked is a great way of figuring out what could be done better, especially when the answer to a question is "I don't know, it's just always been done that way." However, the new hire shouldn't *only* be using their onboarding buddy as a resource for all their questions: they should be attempting to answer their own questions when possible. For example, if there's a company wiki or knowledge base, they should be expected to search for some basics before taking time away from someone else who might just reply with the link to the relevant page themselves. The buddy is great for all the questions that likely won't have written answers though. Things like "Do people eat during the company town hall meeting, and if you do are you expected to keep your camera on?"—but maybe, if that's asked a lot, it should be written down too.

Some companies take this even further: Doist arranges "Mentor Trips" where the new hire is flown to a different city to meet their onboarding mentor, where they can work together in person for a week.[1] This can build relationships faster and speed up the onboarding process. While this tactic might not be possible for some companies and individuals, if the new hire lives in the same city as other current employees it could be nice to have an optional in-person get-together! For a period of a few months, I had the chance to meet all newly hired people at Fellow in my hometown when I'd drop off their swag bag in person.

Putting It All Together

The best onboarding plan is one that is thought out early. Even if the content of the team's documentation is less than stellar, it's the fact that emails were sent out ahead of the start date and there's a semblance of a plan that will stick out and make the experience a pleasant one for everyone involved. Logistically, here is how I structure the prestarting process for new engineers at Fellow:

---

[1] https://blog.doist.com/remote-onboarding/

1. **Preparing the onboarding buddy:** At least two weeks before the scheduled start date, I plan out the ideal onboarding buddy and a backup (in case the person doesn't want to, or unexpectedly isn't available). We have a conversation around what's expected of them, and whether any of their existing work needs to be shuffled around to allow them to dedicate the time for it. When they agree, we go over the full onboarding process so that they're aware of each step and aren't learning about it at the same time as the new hire.

2. **Calendar event:** I create a "Welcome Call" calendar event inviting the new hire, their onboarding buddy, and me, for 10am on their start date (or other time, depending on time zones or any existing obligations on their end). Both their personal and new work emails are invited; since access to your company email isn't given until their start date, this allows them to see what's planned while still having access to the info on their new work calendar once they sign in. The calendar event has a link to the videoconferencing platform we'll be using for the Welcome Call, and the description mentions it too so it's clear that this is in fact a call and not just a reminder.

3. **Schedule:** Around the same time that the Welcome Call is scheduled, I send the Welcome Email following the template of the sample found a few pages earlier. I send this as a separate email and not just as an event description for the call to increase its chances of being read—event descriptions aren't always the most visible, and this email can get lengthy.

4. **Meeting agenda:** Once the Welcome Email is written, I make use of our own product and copy it into the meeting notes for the Welcome Call event in Fellow. I put all of my notes in Fellow, which is a meeting note management platform. This allows easy access to the note for everyone on the event without needing to remember to give out any kind of special access or having to scramble to search for it in a sea of documents—it's right there, attached to the calendar. I invite the new hire to this note as a guest user so that they get access to the read-only version before they even start, which means that they can feel prepared going into their first week. In our case, it also means that they get a first peek at what Fellow looks like, which is fun because it's the product that they're joining to help build.

5. **Prepare for week one:** After preparing the schedule for the week and getting all the right communications sent out, there's still a lot to do to make sure that the schedule goes smoothly! We'll talk about this in the next section.

The First Week

We just covered how to communicate the plan for the first week ahead of time to the new hire, but we didn't cover what that first week should actually be! You want to make sure that you're providing enough structure to the week that they have a clear direction and know in general what the goal they're working toward is, but also not keep it *so* structured that they don't have time to get up for walks in the middle of the day, explore things at their own pace, or reach out to their new coworkers to say hi during business hours. If you're doing back-to-back video calls to make sure that they don't feel alone and resemble an office setting, you're doing it wrong—no one wants to have back-to-back video calls all day with people they've just met; it's exhausting.

So what *should* you be doing in the first week? The specifics will vary a lot from team to team, but at a high level your goals should be

- Creating a welcoming environment
- Setting and managing expectations
- Building social connections
- Familiarizing them with the way of working

Let's talk about how to cover each of those items.

Creating a Welcoming Environment

The number one thing to be done here—and it needs to be said because sometimes managers forget to do it—is to let the rest of the team know ahead of time that someone will be joining the team, and when. Fill them in on some details: give their name, pronouns (information that should have been collected in the hiring process), and what their role will be. The atmosphere will feel more welcoming to the new hire when everyone has a bit of context on who they are already, and every interaction doesn't start with "Hi.... And who are you?".

The second most important thing to do is to remind everyone the day that they join that they should be reaching out to say hi and welcoming the person. This is relevant even if there's a team meeting with them scheduled for early in the week where "you'll meet each other anyway." When you're working remotely and someone new joins, it can be easy to fall into the trap of thinking that they won't notice if you don't send them a message to say hi, especially if the company isn't tiny. It's the bystander effect in action, and it couldn't be further from the truth of what's actually going on for them. They're probably going to be receiving far fewer messages than you expect—unless you have a particularly healthy culture on the team and a lot of extroverts. During this time where they likely know no one, receiving messages saying hi will be seen as nothing other than a positive thing. As a manager, it's your job to make sure that people are actually doing this. It's good to establish the expectation of welcome messages when you've announced that someone new will be joining the team, but I've found that the most effective thing is to reach out individually to people on the team throughout the new hire's first day specifically asking if they've had a chance to talk to them yet. Having that personal nudge makes it much more likely that they really will send a message, and eliminates the bystander effect because they've been singled out. It's good to do this spread out throughout the day so that the person doesn't just get a dozen messages in the morning, and instead will have a steady stream of welcoming messages coming in throughout the day to keep them going (and make it easier to reply to them all).

On top of welcoming them through messages, there are some other things you can do to make sure that they feel like you're making an effort to bring them in as a part of the team. One way of doing this is to invite them to some preexisting meetings. If you have a team meeting, this will be an obvious one to add them to—just make sure that before you dive into the agenda topics, you acknowledge the new hire's presence and give them space to introduce themselves. Depending on the size of the team, this is also a great time for everyone else to introduce themselves over video too (this can be a lot to remember, I've seen companies do intros by having everyone create an "About me" page with whatever content they want in the company wiki for self-serve introductions). I also like to invite them to meetings for ongoing projects that the team has: even though it's unlikely that they'll be adding ideas or contributing to the discussion (or even understanding the majority of what's going on at first), it'll give them the chance to better understand team dynamics, and start getting a feel for what we're up to. This can be really valuable in getting people ramped up, and is the type of thing they would normally have access to in an office environment where you're able to overhear discussions and sometimes even see meetings happening through the glass walls of conference rooms.

Setting and Managing Expectations

When you're joining a new company and no one has told you at what pace they expect you to ramp up, it's easy to assume that you aren't doing it fast enough.

I've fallen into this trap many times. I'll join a company, feel bad for not knowing 100% of what everyone else seems to know, and then spend hours and hours after work for the first few weeks reading up on as much as I possibly can so that I can be just as productive as the other developers, as quickly as possible. But as a manager, we know that it takes time to fully ramp up and understand all the business logic that goes into the projects we're building. Chances are that most engineers on the team also don't have all the answers or know each and every intricate detail of the codebase—it just feels like they do, because they've had more time with it and have built up context by virtue of being present for many of the decisions made.

To prevent your new hires from feeling inadequate and quickly burning out from trying so hard to keep up with everyone, set clear expectations around what their contributions should look like for various timeframes. The first set of expectations that I lay out is for the first week, which are written in the Welcome Email from earlier in the chapter. That email outlines that your first week will be mostly shadowing meetings, meeting people and making connections, reading, and signing documents. In our first one-on-one (one of my favorite meeting types, which we'll talk about in a later chapter) which I schedule for the second half of their first week, I set expectations for the next few months. The expectations differ based on their previous experience and how far along they are in their career, but all follow the same general outline: I give them a good idea of what they should be accomplishing by the first two weeks, first month, second, and then third months—including what duties they'll take on, what they're expected to learn, and how much help I expect them to need. I also make it very clear that taking time to close any knowledge gaps and learn about things should be done *during* work hours, and *not* after, because a strong work/life balance is important for mental health, and to avoid burnout (another topic that we'll cover in a later chapter). The new hire will likely also have their own expectations of what the job is or what they would like for it to be, and it's equally important to ask them about that. This is a good time to clear up any misunderstandings and see if there's anything you could do to set them up for success in meeting those expectations.

Working on Building Social Connections

More important than learning about any process or technology that the team uses is getting to actually meet the team and start to form social connections with them.

When you feel comfortable with the people on your team and start to get to know them at a deeper level, everything about work becomes easier: it's easier to go to them to ask for help, it's easier to collaborate, easier to speak up without fearing that they think what we say will be silly, easier to ask for and give feedback, and overall just easier to get things done. Getting to a place where those bonds are strong takes a long time and won't happen in the first week of onboarding, but that first week is the time where it should get started. And just like how when they started it was important to nudge people to introduce themselves and say hi, it's important here to deliberately set up systems to make sure that these relationships start to form. There are two types of relationships to be built, both equally as important: those that form one-on-one between individual coworkers, and those that exist within the team as a group dynamic.

To create those individual connections, we set up "coffee chats" (coffee not required!) between them and the colleagues that they'll be working with—even if infrequently. I like to limit these to one per day so that they can properly focus on the conversation without getting swept up in meeting too many people at once and promptly forgetting who everyone is. These chats don't need to be centered around work topics, and in fact are better for relationship building if they aren't—but it's all dependent on the comfort level of the participants as to how far outside of work life they want to veer. For continuing the chats after the first week, our #coffee-chats Slack channel does all the work! This channel is connected to Donut, a bot which matches people up every week for a social video call. It's especially useful for its ability to match people across different departments, who might normally never cross paths in remote social circles. It lets us meet others at work, better understand the rest of the business, and ultimately makes everyone have more empathy for one another and make better decisions overall because we have more context on what's going on with the other departments.

Tip   Meeting random people one-on-one every week can also be a bit daunting, and even energy draining (especially for those of us who consider ourselves to be more introverted)—there's also the option of using Donut to meet in groups of three, where the onus of carrying the conversation falls on more people and can be less stressful. Plus, you get to meet twice as many people!

The other form of social connections needed is team building. Forming a strong group dynamic means that in times of need, the team knows that they can count on each other. This can start to happen naturally over time with team meetings as long as there's a decent amount of social time built in to them (see Chapter 3 for more on this), but I like to speed up the process by creating more opportunities for social interaction through specific team events.

Some of the types of remote-friendly events I've seen teams do to have fun are

- Playing online games (think drawing and trivia, safe-for-work games that have mass appeal)

- Giving ten-minute funny slide deck presentations on any (non-work) topic of your choosing

- Guest entertainment (magic show, speakers)

- Virtual escape room

- Creative outlet (paint night, drawing, cooking class, gingerbread house decorating, pumpkin carving, …)

My favorite to rotate between are the creative outlets, where we get to show off a little bit of ourselves and have fun with it (and doing something in the physical world can feel so nice after spending all our time writing code and staring at a computer), and virtual games which require a little less energy and brainpower (also something that can feel so nice after spending all our time writing code).

These events should always take place during business hours because team building is work, so it shouldn't be pushed outside of work time. These events also shouldn't be made mandatory (no one likes "forced fun"), and thought should be put into the specific timing of them: as much as people love games, no one wants to spend an hour playing a game when there's a big launch happening two hours later; everyone's mind will be elsewhere, and attendance will be low.

Familiarizing Them with the Way of Working

Last but not least, in the first week that someone is on the team, they should start to get a feel for how the team gets work done and how communication happens.

This is another place where adding them to some of the meetings for ongoing projects comes in handy: they can see how meetings are run, how updates happen, and what (if any) structure the information flow takes before getting their own projects and diving into the deep end. This is also where having team documentation becomes particularly useful. There are two categories of documentation that every engineering team should maintain:

1. **Technical documentation:** How to set up the codebase, architectural decisions, tech specs, environment configurations, how to reference operational dashboards...

2. **Team documentation:** Best practices and expectations around code review, how and when code deploys happen, how to structure a project, team responsibility breakdowns, ...

Many teams have the first one (at the very least in the project's Readme so that engineers can get it set up), but it's less common to have the second—which is possibly more useful than the first, because the answers aren't deducible from the code.

Team documentation is the type of thing that, when set up right, can help the team scale *far faster* than without it. It holds the answers to all the questions that get asked constantly by engineers both new to the team and not, and which can only otherwise be picked up through context and by being on the team for a while.

At Fellow, our engineering team has an entire directory in Confluence where we create a brand-new page every time someone asks the question "How do we do *<thing that you just have to have been around to know>*?". We write out the answer in as much detail as needed to properly answer the question and any obvious follow-ups, and send the link back to the person. We call this "Respond with a link." Yes, it might seem passive aggressive at first (almost like someone replying with a "Let me Google that for you" link), but you're doing everyone a favor by making that answer available to all current and future teammates. If one person asked it, it's likely to come up again. And that's why although it takes a lot longer to answer the single question that way, it ends up saving people time overall to write it out as a post. Once you have a collection of pages that revolve around the same topic, that's when you know to create a subdirectory and group them together.

Over time, you'll end up with a comprehensive guide to every process that the team has, and everyone will be able to search for answers to their questions. This is useful to all team members, but especially to new hires who are able to get up to speed even faster (and get answers to questions they may not even known to have yet).

Tip It's everyone's duty to update this documentation and create new pages as necessary, and that responsibility shouldn't fall on any one person. As a manager, be on the lookout for typically underrepresented engineers being the ones to always take on the job of writing these pages. This is "glue work"[2] that happens on a team and isn't something a lot of companies view as promotion-worthy tasks, but it's invaluable. Make sure that you're properly recognizing the contributions they're making, and that you're encouraging *all* engineers on your team to write and update the documentation.

The technical documentation will typically include a step-by-step guide to getting the project set up locally. Encourage new hires to update this particular documentation if they run into any issues or see anything

---

[2] "Glue work" is a term coined by Tanya Reilly, which she describes in this article: https://noidea.dog/glue

that is out of date—it's very likely that there will be *something*, even if just particularities with issues in newer operating systems. Giving them this task shows that you have confidence in them, and gives them a sense of accomplishment because they're contributing to the team already. It makes the process smoother for whoever comes after them too, because the issues they might run into will have been addressed. It's a great way to make their first week even better before even getting to write code, because of how early they get to make contributions to the team.

Putting It All Together

Nearly everything covered in this section can be condensed into one single "Onboarding Checklist" that's shared with the new hire, their onboarding buddy, and their manager. I like to maintain a template for this purpose to make it quick on our end to get new hires set up for onboarding too, so that we aren't starting from scratch and spending a lot of time putting this together each time someone joins the team. We're always adding to this and updating existing items as the team and processes evolve. The checklist is different from the Welcome Email because it contains action items: it's quite literally a list of tasks to complete that get checked off as they go through them. This document will look different for every team, but it should contain at a minimum

- A welcoming message, reminding them of their team, manager, and onboarding buddy's names and usernames on your messaging platform.

- Team-specific administrative tasks, such as signing up for all the necessary engineering accounts.

- A list of people (including their names and job titles) to reach out to for questions or coffee chats.

- Links to important information hubs like the team wiki, hosted code, or tech docs.

- First steps for the day. This might be getting the development environment set up, or even a list of tickets to choose from as a starting point. It might even be just familiarizing themselves with certain frameworks before diving in.

It can even be helpful to include tasks for the manager or onboarding buddy too! By adding items like "Schedule 1-on-1s" for yourself or "Introduce to the team" for the buddy, it's easier to remember these critical steps, and it makes the onboarding feel more collaborative (as opposed to however one might feel when being handed a list of things to do). We put these checklists in a shared space where it's easy to drop in and see how things are progressing. Instead of constantly asking the new hire if they're stuck on anything or where they're at, a quick glance at the checklist will show how they're getting through the day without interrupting their flow.

Beyond Week One

Just because the first week is over doesn't mean that onboarding is done! It takes much, much longer than that for any new hire to become a team member that contributes at their full capacity. And it usually takes a long time to properly absorb all of the information as well. Reading through documentation is one thing, putting it to practice and writing code is another.

One-on-Ones

In their first week, set up a recurring one-on-one between the two of you. My preference is to run these weekly for one hour for the first month or so, because there will be a lot of questions and context to give—and lots of getting to know each other to do!

Outside of that one-on-one, check in with them at least once per day just to say hi, or to make sure they're doing alright with the information. When you reach out, it's easier for them to open up and ask any questions that may have been pestering them, because they won't feel like they're pulling you away from other work since they already have your attention.

Simple Tickets

Otherwise, it's really important for the first few months that you've laid expectations for them around how they should be progressing, and what they should actually be doing.

They probably won't be thrown into a large and complex project right off the bat, but they also shouldn't be just sitting around sifting through the code aimlessly for weeks: pretty soon after they join, they need some tasks so that they can work toward a goal and start directing their learning in some way. I like to have a list of tickets that are in increasing complexity for them to work on, and which cover a good cross section of the code so that they're learning as much as possible. They start out on the simplest of tasks: update some text here or a color there. Things that don't require a lot of business logic knowledge to accomplish, but that do give them some insight into where the code for different visual components lives. They're also pretty simple, because at least in the case of text changes you can (usually) just search over the codebase for the old text so that it can be replaced, instead of sifting through many files looking for it manually and working backward and forward through the different components. Their onboarding buddy will also be available to help them through any difficulties.

Deploying Code

After those simple tickets, we walk them through how to deploy code.

We happen to have a simple process where pushing a button deploys all the code, so it's low risk for new hires to run the release. But we still all gather on a Slack Huddle (voice call) together and have them share their screen so we can walk them through it from start to finish—there are still other elements to it, like making sure that the servers are still up after the deploys, and posting release notes. It's empowering for them to be able to do something so large that affects so many people. We aim to do this in their first week on the team and include some code they've written so that they can go into the weekend happy about their new job, and excited for the work that's to come.

In the second week and moving forward, the tickets get increasingly more complicated: maybe some new functionality like showing confirmation messages on actions, or making an interface a little more responsive than before, and then working up into things that tackle business logic and start to get into the nitty-gritty. During all of this, they'll be learning about how to structure pull requests, what the expectations around testing are, and will be setting up their email filters and adjusting notification settings when the many emails from various services start to come in.

Pull Requests

Instead of just reviewing their code, make sure that they're also tagged as reviewers for other people's code changes so that they can get a feel for how it's done by those who have been on the team for a while.

If you have expectations around the language and tone of code review comments, or even the lead time you have between being assigned one and having to review it, that should all be documented in the team documentation system that we talked about earlier. Be on the lookout for their very first pull request, so that you can properly celebrate it! Depending on whether they like receiving public praise or not, you can call it out in the team messaging channel or message them directly telling them they did a great job (or even as a mix of the two, comment on it directly and throw some happy emojis onto it too to really show the excitement at their contribution).

The Importance of Feedback

Onboarding should be an ever-evolving process that is continuously updated. Many of those updates will come from the needs of the team changing, but the most important updates will come from the feedback that the new hires provide about what's working well, and what could use improvement.

At the end of their first week, I send all new hires a feedback survey with just a handful of questions to rate how their week went. This is to judge the usefulness of the content of the onboarding checklist, the way they were welcomed to the team, and whether they had enough support. Most of the questions are star rating questions out of five so that we can easily compare trends over time between process iterations, and two of the questions are optional written answers. This is where we ask what went well and played a major role in their onboarding satisfaction (parts which we should keep), and what was missing or could be improved upon to make it even better for the next person. Our process has been through dozens of iterations, and not once has that second question about what to improve ever been left blank. Even if there's nothing *wrong*, there's always something extra that could be added to go above and beyond, and everyone will have a different idea of what that is. This feedback plays such an important role in how our onboarding takes shape.

Not only should you be requesting feedback, you should also be giving feedback too! Giving positive feedback to the new hire as they work through the onboarding steps and ask questions shows that they're on the right track and are progressing at the right speed—something that they'll be unsure of for at least the first few weeks on the job.

Takeaways from This Chapter

- Even if your organization has a generic onboarding process for employees, you need to set up a specific process for the people joining your team so that they can get up to speed on the job-specific duties they'll be performing.

- Start communicating with the new hire at least a week before their start date. Send them a message with an outline of their schedule for the first week, including a start time on Monday (and how to "show up" to work), and all the meetings they'll be attending and what they need to prepare (probably only an introduction).

- Don't copy the in-office experience by dropping them into video calls all day. No one likes that!

- Make sure that everyone on the team reaches out to say hi to them by personally asking everyone to; otherwise, there will be the bystander effect, and many will not reach out at all. Make sure that introductions go both ways!

- Manage expectations around where they should be at with their learning and by when, so that they don't feel overly stressed and spend all their free time doing research and trying to catch up to be as productive as everyone else immediately.

- Build social connections both individually and within the larger team by using a tool like Donut to schedule coffee chats weekly, and scheduling virtual team events.

- Introduce them to the team's way of working by inviting them to meetings early on, and having a robust set of both technical and team documentation to read from to answer both code- and process-related questions.

- Writing documentation is typically a role taken on by underrepresented minorities in tech. It's critical work but can tend to go unappreciated during promotion time. Make sure that work is being distributed equally among team members, and that the contributions to the documentation are properly recognized.

- Assign them increasingly difficult tasks so they start off feeling great and then get a feel for the business logic in the code. Make sure to celebrate their first pull request, and aim to have them deploy code (or equivalent) within their first two weeks so that they can feel like they're really accomplishing something and that they made the right choice joining your team.

CHAPTER 3

Meetings

When a previously office-based team moves to remote work, a common way of adapting is to fill everyone's calendars with so many meetings that no one actually has enough time to get any "real" work done during the week. There's a thought that if you can't *see* work being done, *no* work is being done.

Don't be *that manager*.

Just as they did in the office, engineers need a lot of time for deep focus when they're writing and reviewing code, writing tech specs, and planning their work out. There's this concept of the manager's schedule vs. the maker's schedule: makers (engineers in this case) need their meetings to be grouped together and few in number. When there's a meeting in the middle of the day, it can throw their schedule off entirely: you don't want to get too deep into a problem when you know you're going to be pulled away from it within an hour, so you don't focus too strongly on anything. And then after the meeting, you need to cool down from the interaction and then work back up into problem-solving mode—hopefully before the end of the day.

Poorly placed meetings can take away hours of productivity, so their timing and purpose should be thought about very carefully. The manager's schedule on the other hand is probably all too familiar: there are many meetings and many interruptions all scattered across your schedule with little to no time to ramp up to any sort of problem that requires intense focus like programming does. But that's okay, because it's not typically

© Alexandra Sunderland 2022
A. Sunderland, *Remote Engineering Management*,
https://doi.org/10.1007/978-1-4842-8584-8_3

your job to do that; it's your job to be interrupted and be available to help people out, and do the types of tasks that don't typically require that level of dedicated focus time. As a manager, when you're scheduling team meetings or other meetings that require developer presence, you should first ask yourself if they truly need (or want) to be there. Then make sure that you're scheduling them at a time that doesn't distract them from that focus. Sometimes, this is inevitable, especially when you have people spread across multiple time zones, and it's going to happen in the middle of the day for *someone*.

Meetings should not be set up as a way to just make sure that work is happening and try to replicate in-office discussions, because of that large disruption to the day. A meeting is also something that takes away from one of the benefits of working remotely, which is that you can be out and about doing things during the day and not necessarily always at your computer. When you do have meetings though, you should always put in the effort ahead of time to make sure that they're as productive as possible and aren't wasting anyone's time. There's an art to this, and it involves honing a lot of skills in preparation, goal setting, moderating, and note taking. Virtual and in-person meetings have a lot in common, but the skills required are a tad different for the former, so we'll cover exactly how to schedule a terrific virtual meeting in the following section before diving into how to host a variety of different and very important meeting types.

How to Schedule a Great Meeting

The tone for the meeting is set long before it even starts: every detail of the scheduled event is so important, from the list of attendees to the amount of time being allocated to it. Here are the things that you have to be aware of when scheduling a virtual meeting between colleagues.

Name/Description

The wording around the event has to clearly communicate its intent and any intended outcomes. Poor naming can confuse—or worse, worry—the people who are invited to it. If you as a manager send an event invitation out of the blue to someone on your team and call it "Let's talk," without any further context, the first thing that goes through their mind is that they're in trouble and possibly on the verge of being fired—even if you might have meant it as a "Let's talk and catch up about our weekends" type of casual conversation. Similarly, if you're meeting with a group of people to solve a problem related to some project you're working on, don't just call the meeting "Problem solving meeting." Titles need to be specific so that when you see the event on your calendar a few days later, you understand what you'll be talking about.

Attendees

The list of meeting attendees is important in conveying what will be happening in the meeting and what the overall tone is. If you invite a large group, say seven or more people, that can send a signal to people that it *might* be okay for them to skip out on the meeting, or not pay attention to it too much since there are so many other people who could be potentially participating at the same time. This is especially a problem with remote meetings, because no one can see what you're doing on your computer while you're in the meeting: if you have a lot of attendees, it's easy to start browsing the internet or catching up on email. If the meeting involves managers and at least one of their direct reports, consider the dynamic that may be creating: if this is a brainstorming or feedback session, the manager's report may not feel totally comfortable speaking up and giving their true thoughts for fear of looking silly.

Date/Time

When scheduling a meeting in person, there are certain physical constraints over the date and time of a meeting: you need to make sure that there's a physical meeting room available that's large enough to host everyone and all the required technology, and it needs to be close enough to whatever meeting room the attendees may have previously been in during the last meeting block, so that they aren't rushing across a building to make it on time. Luckily for us, those constraints aren't there for remote work, but some new ones do exist! Spending hours back to back on video calls can be particularly exhausting, usually more exhausting than when meeting in person, so you'll want to be conscious of what peoples' schedules look like before booking them in for yet another meeting. Maybe adding another hour to the block of four hours isn't such a good idea, and there should be a bit of a break in between. If you aren't sure if an event should be recurring, start by scheduling it for just two or three sessions (you can stop recurring events automatically after a number of occurrences in most calendar providers, like Google or Office). If after the second occurrence it feels like you really need to meet again, then the meeting can be scheduled at that point. It's much easier to schedule more meetings than it is to realize that they should be cancelled, because people will always find a way to fill the void and speak during the time, and it's possible that it could have been done over messaging asynchronously[1] instead.

---

[1] An asynchronous meeting is one where the participants don't meet on a call at the same time, and instead consume the information being disseminated on their own time. It's most useful for one-to-many informational meetings. It's the counterpart to the synchronous meeting.

Length

Meetings are like a gas—they'll fill up as much time as is allotted to them. Err on the side of scheduling meetings to be slightly shorter than the amount of time you might think you need. A good agenda and a strong moderator should be able to keep everyone on track so that the main decisions that need to be made are covered, and all discussion topics have been brought up. If you have a meeting scheduled for two hours or more (this should be extremely rare), you'll have to factor in time for people to get up partway through for a few minutes of break time. A good tactic to implement for creating events is to always end the event 5–10 minutes before the top of the hour. For example, what would normally be a 30-minute event should be 25, and what would normally be a 60-minute event should be 50. This built-in break gives people a few minutes to rest up before what might be another block of meetings. Those empty blocks of time should not be seen as potential overflow for the meeting if it doesn't end on time though: they should be treated as the true end of the meeting.

At Fellow, we have a saying, "No Agenda, No Attenda," and we live by it. If there's no agenda set for a meeting, the meeting probably shouldn't be happening at all. Meetings are very expensive tools to disseminate information and gather opinions: their cost can be measured with the hourly rate of every person attending, plus the ramp-up/ramp-down time around the meeting, and any lost productivity (especially those working on the maker's schedule). They should be scheduled sparingly, and they should be structured in such a way that they're very useful and wouldn't have been better off being done asynchronously. There are a lot of types of meetings that can be done fully asynchronously, for example, the "presentation" meeting: if there's a slide deck involved and someone will be talking to the group for the most part, then a better solution than gathering everyone onto a call together and pulling them away from the work would be to record the presentation and make it available to them all to watch whenever works best for them. This is my favorite way of doing it, because that allows you to watch it back at 2x speed and finish up the content more quickly. If there are questions or there's meant to be a bit of a discussion after, a Slack channel can be created to capture all of that. If at that point there's something that truly would be better off being discussed through speaking, a meeting can be scheduled.

This asynchronous style of meeting is a method used by Loom (a video recording and sharing platform) for their all-hands meetings,[2] whose employees share prerecorded Loom videos instead of presenting live on a call. They've seen many other benefits from converting meetings to this format other than the obvious time-saving ones, like being able to pause or rewatch sections of content, providing presenters with better feedback (through timestamped emojis and comments on their videos), and using the recordings to build up a database of presentations for future employees to watch. While not all meetings can (or should) be run fully as a series of videos, this combination of asynchronous updates with synchronous discussion is a great pairing for remote work.

There are a few different types of meetings that engineering teams need to run, and can be handled in very different ways when done remotely. This isn't an exhaustive list, but the techniques outlined in the examples that follow can be used as bases and adapted to work for any other type of meeting you may be scheduling.

Team Retrospectives/Brainstorming

Retrospectives are some of my favorite meetings to run! I run them with the entire engineering team at Fellow twice per year, once in June and once in December before we all go on break. We've been on this twice-yearly cadence for years, and have built up some really great remote-first habits out of it that influence the rest of our meetings. Retrospectives are an

---

[2] www.loom.com/blog/asynchronous-meeting

important tool for engineering managers to better understand the team's concerns that might not be brought up day to day, and work together to make real changes so that the team is constantly improving over time.

The very first retrospective we ran was in person. We booked the boardroom for four hours in the afternoon, and I brought a box filled with sticky notes, markers, stickers, and cookies and chocolate—for the extra energy we'd need. After talking through the goal of the retro and the parameters (basics such as don't be mean, and comment on process and results instead of people) we spent the first 20 minutes silently writing our thoughts on the sticky notes, and awkwardly looking up every so often to see if others were done or if we could peek and get some inspiration from the things they had written down. Eventually, we all got up and put our sticky notes on the wall where we had defined three categories: Good, Bad, and Ugly. The idea here is that we wanted to break things down so that we'd talk about what's going really well on the team, what issues are coming up that will need to be addressed at some point, and what are issues *right now* that we need to solve ASAP. We crowded around this board putting up our notes, and then with our little dot stickers, read through each and every sticky note, grouping similar ones together, and adding dots to those that we agreed with. There were a dozen people squished together trying to decipher scribbly handwriting, and trying to somehow move down the wall and read everything in the ten minutes allotted, without getting in each other's way. Once all the dot stickers were up, we took a step back to form a semicircle around the wall and started to mentally map out which notes had the most popularly held thoughts and concerns. We spent the next three hours together reading through every sticky note one by one, asking whoever had written it to give more context and often having two or three conversations happening in the group all at once to discuss it. It was chaotic! We started with the "Good" and moved toward the "Bad," but by the end when we reached the "Ugly" sticky notes, we were so tired that we just agreed that the items need addressing, and that we'll talk about how to address them later—somewhat defeating the purpose of this entire afternoon exercise. Not all retrospectives need to involve creating solutions though, it can be beneficial to use them as a way of getting thoughts and concerns off your team's chest, without everyone worrying about needing to bring a solution for everything they mention (which could deter them from bringing up what's really on their minds).

The feedback received in the post-retro survey was that everyone had fun, the cookies were great, but it was *far too long*. So for our very first retro as a remote team, we went with what we knew, and ran it in the exact same way that we had before, using Miro as a virtual whiteboard with sticky notes to replace our physical one. And instead of four hours, it would only be three.

It was not fun.

This time, we renamed the Good/Bad/Ugly categories to Squirrel/Mouse/Rat, chosen by an engineer on the team who had recently immigrated to Canada, and adored all the squirrels running around the streets which didn't exist where he lived before. That was probably the best part of the retro. Running the retro remotely with Miro solved a lot of the in-person issues that we had been running into before: it was so much easier to understand what was written (no more deciphering handwriting), everyone could see each other's virtual sticky notes as they were being written, no one had to get up and crowd around a wall, and the emoji button on the sticky notes counted how many reactions there were so we wouldn't have to guesstimate. But what we found was that three hours in a virtual meeting is not the same thing as three hours in person. We tried to make it more interactive by having different moderators for each section, but it became difficult for everyone to concentrate when it was so easy to become distracted by other things going on on our laptops. Even with a ten-minute break in the middle, we still all spent such a long time on this one call that I'm fairly certain everyone shut their laptop and collapsed on their beds afterward—I know I did.

After a lot more feedback and a few more iterations on the remote retro format, we finally landed on something that works extremely well. We're able to all stay focused, have good discussions, *and* come up with proper action items and solutions during our time together. And we don't need to spend half the day on a video call!

The key to a great virtual retrospective is to embrace the best parts of remote work. Copying the usual methods for in-person retros will leave you with people feeling disassociated from the meeting, not paying attention, and not wanting to do another one (which is a shame, they're so useful!). I found that building retros with both *asynchronous* and synchronous portions led to the best discussions, and the happiest team. We don't all have to be sitting in the same room (physical or virtual) to think of and write ideas, or to read through them, or even to vote on them. The only activity that really requires people to be present at the same time is the deep, nuanced discussions. It's absolutely possible to have those kinds of discussions over text, but there's much more energy and enthusiasm when people get to talk through issues and bounce ideas off each other in real time (when they aren't tired from being on a call for three hours already).

Here's how we structure our retrospectives now.

Days 1–2: Asynchronous

Everyone writes down their thoughts for each category in a common space. You can use tools like Miro or Figma for board-like visualization of ideas. We use the meeting note for the event in Fellow, which gives us the ability to comment, react, move items around, and easily create and track any resulting action items within the tools we already use.

These few days are solely for brainstorming, and replace the 20 minutes that you would spend silently together doing this. By having it spread across a few days, it allows people to add items as they come up, write when it's most convenient for them in the day, and spend quite a bit more time thinking.

Tip for Other Meetings   Sharing ideas and discussion topics before a synchronous meeting happens isn't just useful for retros! It's important to always create an agenda for any meeting where decision-making or brainstorming discussions will take place—it turns the call into a more productive use of time because participants have the chance to think things through ahead of time instead of on the call all together.

Days 3–4: Asynchronous

Once all the items are in the shared virtual space, everyone can start to vote on them (whether that be with virtual stickers or emoji reactions), and start discussions by writing comments. Often in retros, there will be points that either don't require discussion at all (as is often the case for the "Good" category) or where the discussion is straightforward and can be done asynchronously through writing. Those types of items have a tendency to take a lot longer to get through when speaking on a call because people want to provide explanations, so by commenting on them and "wrapping them up" before the call, you end up saving everyone a lot of time and leave more energy to focus on the discussion-heavy topics.

Because this portion is being done asynchronously over the course of a few days, everyone has more time to think about the larger issues and either figure out how they feel about it, collect data, or start coming up with solutions. You don't get that benefit with in-person retros, where the topics on sticky notes are presented just a few minutes before you start talking through them, leaving little time to process them. This gives a huge advantage to the actual conversation, because the amount of thought that's gone into each item makes the conversations move along at a faster pace, and with better ideas.

The last part of this step happens right before the retro call itself: setting an order to the items so that the most important (and popular) items are talked about first. There's a bit of an art to this, and the ordering is vaguely based on how critical each item appears to be, how many votes it received, and what the discussion on it has been like so far. It'll likely be obvious which items really need to be discussed, and which don't necessarily need to be talked about right away.

Day 5: Synchronous

This is the big day, the retrospective itself! This is where you'll schedule a video call with everyone involved. I find the sweet spot length for retro calls to be 90 minutes: just long enough to stay interested the whole time, just short enough to not require a scheduled break (individuals walking away for a few minutes is always okay, of course). This is a far cry from the four hours that we were originally scheduling! The timeline is short, but it keeps you focused and on track because you know that there's a lot to get through—when you have too much time available, it's easy to end up spending far too long on each individual item because "there's so much time." Many of the time-consuming tasks have also already been taken care of in the asynchronous portion: if your team has prepared by reading all the talking points beforehand, everyone should be ready to dive into discussion.

We start with a quick overview of the "Good" section to get everyone warmed up and into the right mindset, and then get right to the "Bad" category which has already been organized to showcase the most important topics. Ahead of time, determine how much time to dedicate to each section so that you can keep track of time and avoid running out of time before getting to the really important topics. Do not go over time with this meeting; any more than 90 minutes and everyone's attention will start to wane!

During the retro, there are a lot of jobs to be done. There's the role of the moderator (possibly you) who makes sure that the right items are being discussed, moves things along when they're dragging on, and ensures that everyone is able to participate (there's no one subset of people dominating the meeting). There's also the note taker, who writes down the main points, decisions, and action items. We've found it best to decide on whether we want to come up with solutions or push discussions to later while we're still talking about each point. We used to recap at the very end of the whole retro to figure this out for each item, but by then we had all forgotten the context behind the sticky notes which made it feel like our earlier discussions had wasted time. Before moving on from one item to the next, decide as a group whether it's something that requires further discussion (and decide who will arrange that discussion and who will be involved), or whether it's something that you have a solution for right now—in which case, write that solution down before you forget! At the very end of the retro, recap over those decision notes. It's a good way to make sure that nothing was missed, and gives a sense of accomplishment and feeling that the last 90 minutes were a good use of everyone's time.

Tip for Other Meetings   Many meeting types result in action items being discussed, not just retrospectives. Unfortunately, it's all too common for the group to agree that something must be done, and move on in the conversation without being clear about who should do it. Whenever it's decided in a meeting that something must be done, always write it down and clarify *who* will be completing that task, and by *when*. This one habit will prevent many misunderstandings!

By structuring the retro in this async/sync fashion, it's easier for more people to participate than if it were entirely synchronous. If you're doing the "everyone creates virtual stickies at the start of the meeting" style of retro, things can get crowded pretty quickly. There's a lot of movement on the board, many opinions to be heard, and a lot of information to sift through to figure out what should be talked about first. When the first portion is asynchronous, the information can be digested over time, which makes it easier to understand and less overwhelming. Since more discussions can happen through the comments, there are fewer things that need to be talked about out loud. It overall allows for more voices to be heard because it reduces so much of the noise.

The retrospective isn't over after hanging up the call, there are still things to do! The first thing to do is send out a recap to everyone who was involved, detailing what decisions were made, and what action items came out of it. This can be in an email, in the team Slack channel, or whatever medium will actually be seen by the participants. Make sure those action items are actually followed up on, and maybe even set a reminder for yourself to check up on them the week after. Retros are great for getting things off your chest, but the true benefit is in making positive change on the team—and that's more likely to happen if the decisions made are followed through on.

Tip for Other Meetings   The recap of the retrospective doesn't only need to be sent to the people who were on the call. Meeting recaps are a great tool for keeping people informed about discussions and decisions, without them needing to dedicate time to being on a call.

Lastly, send out a feedback survey to everyone who participated. I like to use the same set of questions every time so that I can track the overall trend between each session, and I add a few custom questions based on whatever new methodology we're trying out at the moment. I ask questions like

- How useful did you find this retro?

- Would you want to participate in another retro in a few months?

- What did you think about the length of time we spent on the call?

This is the "retro after the retro," and it's the most powerful tool you have in making them successful. Every iteration we've done on the format and timing of our retrospectives has come out of comments from that survey where people are honest, and it's improved them *so much*. If we didn't collect that feedback, I don't think we'd still be doing them because they would have become so tiresome, and four hours long.

Once the feedback is collected, summarize, anonymize, and share it with the team. Sharing feedback in that way builds trust, and honestly, they're going to be curious as to what everyone else thought too. When it's shared, also share whether there are any changes that are going to be implemented for the next retro based on it. Showing that you truly appreciate honest feedback and will act on it will only encourage people to give their feedback in the future too, and it will go a long way to building a healthy team culture.

Tip for Other Meetings   Collecting regular feedback about all the meetings that you run is a healthy habit. Participants won't necessarily offer up their unsolicited opinions, but will answer specific questions about the meeting when asked! Feedback about components such as length, discussion topics, and meeting moderation will fast-track the meeting's evolution and turn it into an even better use of everyone's time.

Team Building

One of the big concerns of teams that make the switch to remote work, and of people considering joining a remote team, is how the team will feel like a real team and get work done in a great way.

People who worked in an office may be used to having regular hangouts with their team where they go out for lunch often, play ping pong tournaments, and have a midday tea break where they swivel their chairs around and talk about the things going on in their lives. The worry is then, without being able to do that, how will everyone become friends? Hot take: you don't need everyone to be friends to have a functional and effective team! You *do* need everyone to get along though—but the two are very different from each other. Teams that perform the best are teams that have a high level of trust among all the members. They trust that they'll all communicate with each other, that they'll produce high-quality work, and that they'll be there for each other when things go wrong. This trust is something that can naturally evolve over time, but it will take a long time, and a lot of working together to get there. Depending on what type of team you have, that may not even ever happen (e.g., if everyone is on the same team but always working on very disjoint projects with little interactivity between each one). This is by no means a replacement for actually working together though. No amount of fun activities will fix the relationships in a team if someone is constantly underperforming and not delivering on their work.

So what types of team building events should you run? There are many options! First and foremost, team building events should always be run during the normal workday. If there are events scheduled after the normal core work hours, people may feel pressured to attend when they would otherwise be off doing other things (like attending to dependents, going to classes, or otherwise just living their lives which doesn't revolve around work), and it's putting them in a not-so-great spot if they're the only ones on the team that don't attend the event—that might make them look like they aren't team players, which isn't a fair assumption to be making. If your team is spread across multiple time zones, it's likely that you have at least one synchronous team meeting on a recurring basis: you can replace one of those meetings with a team event.

There are a lot of types of team building events, and it's good to switch them up often so that they don't get too repetitive. It's also good to tailor the event to the mood of the team at the time. For example, if the team just spent months back to back working intensely to get a major project out, everyone is probably feeling pretty tired, and maybe doing a brain-intensive thing like a virtual escape room wouldn't be the best idea. But if they just spent a lot of time doing some extremely boring refactoring work (like adjusting all the text strings in the codebase to be internationalization ready), then maybe they could use something a little more creative to do. Here's a list of some of the best team building events I've seen companies do.

Games

The most obvious of them all. There are many, many sites that offer free games to play as a group while not colocated. It's best to choose one that doesn't require any particular skill or prior knowledge, so everyone can equally have fun without feeling left out (i.e., don't play an FPS game or something "gamers" would play). The best games are those that don't require an account or downloads to play, last up to 15 minutes, and require little energy to play, so that in case people need to drop in and out throughout the session, it isn't causing a big disturbance. Opting for a game that requires intense focus like Monopoly isn't the best idea, unless you're an ultra-ambitious team.

Escape Rooms

You may be familiar with the popular in-person escape rooms that took North America by storm in the mid-2010s. There are now a myriad of virtual versions of these! The escape room concierge guides the team through the escape room experience over Zoom and a website to solve puzzles to unlock some objective (like making your way to Mars or finding the secret identity of the spy). They're very logic-heavy, so a popular choice for engineers!

Live Creative Experiences

These are a little harder to coordinate with a team because they require some preparation on everyone's end, and can sometimes make assumptions about the space that people have available.

The most popular examples I've seen are painting classes, chef-instructed cooking lessons, and drawing how-tos. For some activities, the team either needs to be sent a package with the required materials or given a list with the expectation that they pick the items up for themselves. For cooking, that expectation extends to assuming that everyone has a proper cooking space for the event. This isn't always possible, for example, when people live with roommates and have a shared kitchen, or if you live in a space with a stovetop but no oven. These events also typically have people encouraging you to keep your camera on for better interaction and so they can see progress, but showing off your kitchen can feel like an invasive look into your home—and can be awkward when there's a pile of dishes behind you. No matter what, the basic materials for these types of creative experiences (food, paint, ...) should be fully covered by the company so that employees aren't out a sum of money just to participate in what can feel like mandatory fun. It's better to cover the cost up front instead of providing reimbursement, because not everyone might have the capacity at the moment to carry that cost for the few weeks it'll take to receive reimbursement.

Done right though, these types of experiences can be extremely valuable in bringing a team together because you're doing something "live" and away from the computer that they probably spend all day on. Hopefully, it's something that everyone is equally new to, so that you have the sense of accomplishment and learning together.

Watch-n-Learn

Probably the easiest one for team members to join, because it requires no planning on their end and not a lot of effort in terms of participation. It's suitable for any time of year, whether or not you're getting out of a heavy workload. Watch-n-learn events are ones where typically an external speaker is brought in to give a presentation for an hour about something they're an expert in. But it doesn't have to be just a slideshow type of presentation! You can have live private magic shows from magicians in Las Vegas, or a talk about the creative process from Disney animators, ... There are many options out there. Choosing something vastly different from engineering is best, so that people are getting exposed to different ideas, and it truly feels like a break from work.

Good Old-Fashioned Social Hour

Not every team building activity needs to revolve around an activity. A lot of the relationship building happens in the downtime between different parts of each session, where team members get to talk with each other. It's perfectly fine to schedule time during the day to just chat! Come prepared with icebreaker questions just in case the conversation needs a little kindling to really get going.

There are many, many other types of subevents that fall into these categories. If you search for "remote team activities," you'll get a myriad of suggestions, some more cheesy than the others. The key is to pick something that the team will enjoy and which actually fosters these connections, and fits in well with the current environment on the team.

A good cadence for team building activities is once per month. Realistically, with vacation planning and holidays, that means that you'll get nine to ten team events per year—the equivalent of just over one day of work. That's like one team offsite! That's not a lot of time to dedicate toward improving relationships on the team, especially when it means better work output and higher morale overall. Instead of trying to figure out a date and time that works every month, set up an event on a recurring schedule so that these are planned automatically. As the manager, you should take on the duty of planning these out, but also make sure to get input from everyone on what types of things they'd like to do (or not do).

The "Stand-Up"

The stand-up meeting is one of the most controversial meetings in the remote work world.

Typically, this is a meeting that happens multiple times per week where everyone on a team gets together (sometimes literally standing up in a circle) and talks about what they accomplished yesterday, what they're going to work on today, and if they have any blockers. Critics of this type of meeting point out that the timing of the meeting forces people to show up to work early (or the early risers to be forced out of their deep work—which, as we talked about with the maker's schedule, is bad), it's long and boring because no one truly pays attention to what everyone is saying, and sometimes it goes on far too long because people start to discuss solutions to problems instead of just providing updates. Fans of stand-ups say that it helps them stay updated on what everyone is working on, and that it's a form of team building. In the remote world, synchronous team stand-up meetings are equally as bad—potentially worse because of the possibly mismatched time zones—but a tad better because *usually* no one will actually force you to *stand up* for them. They're still quite the disruption though! But some say that they're even more necessary than before, because when you can't walk from desk to desk and see people in person, as the manager, how on *earth* will you ever know what's going on? Stand-ups aren't the solution for staying up to date (we'll talk about strategies for this in Chapter 6), but stand-ups (or "team check-ins" as I prefer to call them) in some form do have a place in your team, as long as they're structured properly.

My teams have been doing remote team check-in meetings twice per week for the last few years. I've tried to remove this meeting from their calendars plenty of times, always thinking that everyone must be seething at the thought of having to join it first thing in the morning (10:30am for most). I've asked probably a dozen times, and even sent out anonymous surveys, but the results always come back the same: everyone loves this meeting, and they do not want it to go away. And my team isn't the exception here, this is the case for a lot of other teams that run their check-ins in the same way that we do.

Tip for Other Meetings   Ask the question "Is this meeting still worth having?" for all the recurring meetings that you organize, once per month. Not all meetings need to last forever, and sometimes they go stale. By actively thinking about whether they're still useful, any issues can be course-corrected before veering too far off from the main purpose—or the meeting can be cancelled altogether, freeing up everyone's time.

The trick is to not make the check-in about the work. There should rarely be any surprises in what people say about what they're doing, and it should really just have the purpose of people understanding for themselves what they want to focus on for the day and getting prepped for it. The real benefit that we get out of these meetings is the social time.

Our check-ins are scheduled for half an hour, twice per week, and we spend the majority of that time just talking about non-work topics. On Monday's edition, we talk about what we got up to over the weekend (with lots of recommendations from people on new activities, like a newly discovered Alpaca farm or a fun hike), and on Wednesday's edition, we talk about how our week is going and what we have planned for the upcoming weekend. We're very focused on life in general outside of work, which helps us get to know each other a lot better. No one is ever pressured to share about their own lives, but we all get to enjoy talking together about everything going on. It builds up the team. And this is what people have been saying every time I try to cancel the meetings for what I think is their benefit: they want it to stick around, because they love the social aspect of it. When there's something big going on, a portion of the meeting is spent talking about work specifically. But for the smaller updates, we write out our main two to three points in the agenda for the meeting so that we don't need to go over it out loud together, since it's all written there to be read asynchronously.

Tip for Other Meetings   Just like with the retrospectives, asynchronous communication should be a common theme in remote meetings! As much information as possible (including status updates) should be written ahead in the meeting notes so that little to no time needs to be spent on it on the actual calls for each meeting.

If a team is stretched across too many time zones, it's possible that this type of check-in won't work. But otherwise, it's a nice excuse to talk more with each other and get more team building in, disguised as an official meeting.

Takeaways from This Chapter

- Virtual meetings should be scheduled sparingly, and a lot of attention should be put into the name, timing, and attendee list.

- Meetings are the most expensive tool in your toolkit. They cost in people's salaries and in lost productivity time.

- When scheduling meetings with your direct reports, be aware of how they likely operate on the "maker's schedule" and not the "manager's schedule" like you do. Schedule meetings in blocks and around the start or end of the day so that you don't interrupt their workflow and prevent them from getting into deep work.

- Try to schedule meetings that end 5–10 minutes before the top of the hour (25 minutes instead of 30, or 50 minutes instead of 60) so that people with back-to-back meetings get a built-in break.

- "No Agenda, No Attenda." If you're scheduling time on people's calendars and pulling them away from work, make sure that you have an agenda set for the meeting and that everyone is aware of it so they can prepare. Otherwise, you might end up with some declined invitations!

- Instead of scheduling meetings for presentations, record them ahead of time and distribute them so that people can watch them on their own time (and at double speed).

- Retrospectives are powerful tools for making positive change on your engineering team and making people feel like their voices are being heard. Organize them at a regular cadence.

- Run retrospectives with an async portion for the parts that don't require synchronous collaboration (likely everything except for the deep discussions). This will make the call shorter, allow for opinions and solutions to be thought through, and keep everyone happier.

- Always send recaps after retrospectives and make sure that the assignees of the action items are held accountable. This is as important as the retro itself, because it fosters trust that people are being listened to and that they aren't just a waste of time.

- Your team members don't need to be friends with each other, but they do need to have high trust in order to be a high-performing team. Team building events can accelerate that trust, but are not a replacement for trust built through actual code development.

- Schedule team building events on a recurring basis once per month. You'll end up with about nine to ten hours of dedicated team building per year, which isn't a lot of time overall to put toward fostering higher team morale and relationship growth.

- When planning a team event, keep in mind the level of energy and brainpower required to participate, and whether that meshes with the current output that everyone's likely to be able to contribute (don't schedule an intense virtual escape room if it's crunch time!).

- Team check-ins aren't terrific for status updates (and shouldn't be used as such), but they're great as team building time disguised as an official meeting.

CHAPTER 4

One-on-Ones

The one-on-ones that I have with my team are some of my favorite meetings of the week. I get to hear about what's going on in their lives, support them through decisions or issues they're facing at work, and coach them to help them reach their career goals. They're extremely valuable and enjoyable meetings, but they weren't always like that.

I can clearly remember two distinct periods in time when my one-on-ones were just plain *awkward*: when I first started having them with my manager as an engineer many years ago, and when I started having them with my team of engineers as a manager. In the first case, I didn't understand the purpose behind them—was this a dedicated office hour just for me, to get help with code? We never spent more than a few minutes talking before going back to work. It wasn't until years later when I started to read about what one-on-ones are for and the benefits that they bring that I started to understand their true purpose and come prepared for them. And yet years after that, when I became a manager and started to have one-on-ones from that new point of view, I was thinking "Why isn't anyone bringing things to talk about to our meetings, do they not like me?". This, I learned, wasn't true—everyone just had as little context as I originally had about why one-on-ones are amazing, and how to make the time spent in them as beneficial as possible.

One-on-ones are incredibly valuable no matter what a team's work setup is, but even more so when working remotely. One-on-ones might be the only time that an engineer gets to spend time alone with their

© Alexandra Sunderland 2022
A. Sunderland, *Remote Engineering Management*,
https://doi.org/10.1007/978-1-4842-8584-8_4

manager and bring up topics that might not be appropriate in larger group meetings, and it gives them the opportunity to have time and thought dedicated to whatever it is that they want to talk about. This type of meeting is so fundamental to building relationships with your team members and is critical for success in the manager role that it deserves its own chapter separate from the previous one about meetings. Throughout the chapter, I'll go over the best way of structuring remote one-on-ones, and talk about some of the mistakes that I've made along the way and how to work around those same pitfalls—all which helped turn those one-on-ones I have from awkward to critical.

An Introduction to One-on-Ones

One-on-ones are some of the most common—and yet the most misunderstood—meetings that a manager has.

One-on-ones are meetings held between an employee and their manager, and act as dedicated time for the employees to receive feedback, be coached, work through issues together, and otherwise talk about anything that is on either of their minds. It's a great time to work through topics that shouldn't be discussed in group meetings, and are specific to the direct report. These meetings are extremely important for a multitude of reasons, but the biggest one is

> *An employee's happiness at their job is in large part dictated by their relationship with their manager. One-on-ones are the best tool at your disposal for building and maintaining that bond and trust with each member on your team.*

Building trust with your team members and helping them grow is a fundamental part of being a manager, and so a lot of importance should be placed in making sure that one-on-ones happen often and happen *well*, since they're the easy path to getting there. These aren't meetings that you can go into unprepared for and hope for the best—they require meticulous preparation on both sides to make sure that the right topics are being discussed, you're making the most of the time together, and you're showing that you care. Having them prescheduled on a recurring basis makes sure that you're spending enough time with each direct report each year to be actively helping them in their growth as an employee. If you were to spend just 30 minutes with each member of your team every two weeks, you would be spending at most 26 hours together every year— without counting the meetings cancelled from holidays, vacations, and conflicts. Twenty-six hours is just a little more than three typical workdays per year! In the long run, that's not a large time commitment for such an important part of the job, which makes it even more important to properly prepare for, and avoid cancelling, these meetings—especially when remote, where chance-encounter individual interactions between the two of you probably seldom happen.

The format and way that my one-on-ones are run has changed a *lot* over the years because of the things I've learned away, the changes the companies I've worked at have gone through, the number of people that I manage, the context that I have on their day-to-day work, and where each person is at in their career. No two managers will have the exact same one-on-one style, and no two direct reports will have the same style with their common manager either. They're an extremely personal thing that may even vary in style and format from one week to the next. That's all to say that there's no single "right" way to do one-on-ones, and it will take time to find something that feels comfortable with everyone if you're new to hosting these. With some people that I've managed, we spend most of the time troubleshooting technical issues together and working through implementation details for projects that they're working on. With others, we'll often talk through blue-sky ideas they have for the engineering team's processes. And with others, I'll dive into explaining various aspects of the business. Those and the many other takes on one-on-one topics are all equally valid, and all feel completely natural with each person. The format and topics to be discussed in one-on-ones are limitless!

The Benefits of One-on-Ones

As I talked about earlier, one-on-ones are the most powerful tool at your disposal for building and maintaining relationships and trust with your team members. But what does that actually mean, and how is that trust built? It's not just a matter of showing up at the scheduled time and magically creating that bond effortlessly—the work needs to be put in. And they aren't just useful for creating trust in order to keep retention on the team high! There are many benefits that one-on-ones bring for both managers and their direct reports.

Benefits for the direct reports:

- They have dedicated time to receive individualized feedback.

- They can speak more freely about their opinions, or ask questions they would be uncomfortable asking in front of the team.

- Their manager is focused on them and what they have to say, without needing to fight for airtime to speak in meetings with very vocal participants.

- There's time set aside to be coached in areas in which they're trying to grow.

- Any sensitive topics that might be tough to bring up in any other context can be talked about privately here.

- The time can be used to better understand priorities, business context, or other things that will help them accomplish their work.

Benefits for the manager:

- Feedback about various initiatives or changes to the team can be collected, and questions can be answered in a private setting. One of my favorite topic formats to use in one-on-ones is "What do you think of <*thing that happened, presentation that was given, or new initiative*>?". I also like to ask them engineering-specific questions like what they think is missing from our roadmap, or what tech debt they're seeing that they think we need to address sooner rather than later.

- Issues can be discovered proactively. People will be more likely to bring up issues that aren't big *yet* but *will* be in conversation than they will be to mention it in out of the blue on Slack, for example.

- It can be a pulse check on how the team is doing overall. Whether it's something going on in their personal lives or the world which is taking a toll on their ability to concentrate, or a particular project is dragging them down and they could use a break, understanding how everyone is doing allows managers to make better decisions around the workload for the team.

- It's a preset time to give feedback. As we'll go over in Chapter 7, it's important to give timely feedback—but not all feedback needs to be delivered immediately. One-on-ones are a great time to deliver feedback, and for follow-up as necessary. Having this time set aside takes away the stressful factor of messaging someone "Do you have time for some feedback?".

- Their cadence creates structure for the other manager-employee relationship tasks that you should be running. For example, progress on any goals that have been set should be checked in on every six weeks or so. Having one-on-ones on a weekly or biweekly cadence already in place means that every third or sixth one-on-one could have part of the agenda reserved for reviewing those goals, instead of needing to remember to check in on them separately.

- Last but not least, the team feels more engaged. Getting face time with your manager means that you're more likely to have them notice your accomplishments, and you get more of a chance to grow in your career. And over time, you start to learn more about each other—whether it's details of each other's personal lives, communication preferences, or a general sense of how you think, everything adds up and helps to create that relationship that trust is built on.

No matter which way you look at it, one-on-ones are clearly beneficial to the manager-employee relationship, which carries through to the health of the whole team.

Remote One-on-Ones

One-on-ones themselves aren't a remote-specific practice, but their value increases quite a bit when teams are remote as opposed to being in an office together. As with all the topics we've seen in the previous chapters, there are some key differences between the in-person and remote versions of them too! And just like everything else—one-on-ones are even *better* in the world of remote work.

Why One-on-Ones Are Better When Remote

Me saying that remote one-on-ones are better than their in-person counterparts might sound counterintuitive for a meeting that's meant specifically to build connections—I know. But there are some key aspects of remote work that allow for one-on-ones done over video calls from home to be even more powerful. I love a good in-person one-on-one (I remember one day in August where I did all my one-on-ones in a park and bought us both ice cream for each meeting, it was quite the day), and I'll still do the odd "walking one-on-one" with those on my team who live nearby, but they don't quite compare to the long-term relationships that we've built up remotely.

Notably, remote one-on-ones give the following benefits:

- **The process of getting to them is *far* less awkward:** You join the videoconferencing platform, and you're there. In an office, it's likely that your seat is in the same area as your team's—which means that when it's time for a one-on-one, you both get up at the same time and walk together to some meeting room just to close the door and talk more privately. It feels almost clinical, and very formal.

- **You have far more options in terms of location for where you'll be conducting the one-on-one:** In an office, you might be in a glass-walled conference room with poor soundproofing—that can make it tough to bring up sensitive or emotional topics, because others might easily see or hear what's going on. Doing a one-on-one from home means that you know exactly who can and can't overhear what you're saying, and it's likely none of your coworkers. If there are really important but tricky issues, you'll be more likely to hear about them from your team when remote because of this, because they have that privacy.

- **You can make yourself more comfortable:** This doesn't necessarily mean having the perfect desk setup, and it means different things for different people. For me, it means being able to sit cross-legged on my chair with a blanket, a mug of coffee, and fidgeting with whatever is on my desk. This helps me concentrate and really focus on what I'm hearing, but isn't the look I'd necessarily want to go for in an office—it works remotely, because no one can see. When people feel more at ease, they share their opinions more openly. It will make the time spent in one-on-ones even more valuable because you'll be more likely to get to the real substance of discussion topics together.

There are many other reasons too, for the most part revolving around the theme of physical and emotional comfort with interacting over video instead of in person—like how much easier it is to carry a conversation without needing to think about making eye contact during tough subjects, or being able to take note and look at your own notes when delivering feedback. This of course isn't a universal experience, and some people thrive more in true face-to-face interactions. In a perfect world, there would be a healthy mix of one-on-one time done both remotely and in person where possible.

How to Structure Your One-on-Ones

There are two core components to think about when setting up one-on-ones: the scheduling of them and their agendas.

There are a few key aspects to scheduling one-on-ones: how long they are, at what point in the week they take place, and their frequency. All three of those parts are very personalized to the team, and there's no one approach that will work best for everyone. I've gone through many iterations of each as the team and my role evolves, and depending on how much support everyone needs from me. In my last iteration of one-on-one scheduling with a team of four, I had asked each person what time of day and which day of the week works best for them to meet, and since everyone had different answers, I had one-on-ones scheduled all over the place in my calendar. Some of them were biweekly because people didn't need as much support, and some were twice as long as the others. Each specific meeting had been tailored to each person on my team, which was great for them because it allowed them to use their best focus time on writing code. But by the time my team expanded to eight people, this strategy of working around their preferences wasn't possible anymore, and I had to start from scratch. I cancelled all of the one-on-ones, and rebuilt the events to work best for me—which at that new point in time was in both of our interests: I would have to do less context switching and be in the same headspace for everyone on the team, which meant that they would have a more present manager in their one-on-one time. In the new iteration, each one-on-one is 45 minutes long, once every two weeks, on Thursday afternoons. I start each one on the hour so that we have a 15-minute buffer between each, giving time to go over if needed, and a break in between if not. In a few months, I'm sure that this will change again, and that's okay! The most important part is that they happen, and they happen often.

The only must-haves when scheduling your one-on-ones are

- They need to be at least 30 minutes long.

- They should preferably be weekly, and at most biweekly.

- They should almost never be cancelled or moved.

Tip   To avoid easily preventable one-on-one cancellations, don't schedule them for Mondays or Fridays. Those are the two days that are most likely to be holidays, and most likely to be taken to extend long weekends. By scheduling one-on-ones for Tuesday, Wednesday, or Thursday, there will be far less last-minute cancellation or event moving that needs to take place.

Having a written and well-prepared collaborative agenda that each participant has access to ahead of the meeting is vital to successful one-on-ones—we'll get more into this in the next section. But what should actually be on the agenda? One-on-ones can be some of the hardest meetings to prepare agendas for because there's no single narrow topic like there is for most other meetings, and it instead can contain discussions that revolve around anything that remotely has to do with the direct report.

There's common advice given around one-on-one agendas that the *vast* majority of the discussion topics should be coming from the report, and the *vast* majority of the talking should be done by them too—to the point where it's 90% them, 10% the manager for each. While the intent behind this advice is good (being that the meeting is for the report, and they should be using the time to their advantage), I strongly disagree with the advice itself. I don't think that the majority of the burden of creating the agenda should be put on the direct report; I think that the responsibility of making sure that the appropriate topics are being discussed should be placed equally on them and their manager. One-on-ones should be very collaborative meetings that the manager is putting a lot of effort into, and not just acting as a resource for answering whatever questions their team has and helping sort out their weekly priorities. The topics that the manager does add should be beneficial though, no status update requests and the like. I put a lot of thought into each one-on-one so that I come prepared with discussion items that will help my team, whether it's growth opportunities I've found for them, things I want their opinion on, or ideas on how they could contribute to the team.

I find that this way of structuring the one-on-one agendas creates a more equal meeting, and doesn't leave people scrambling to find things to talk about with their "boss." It helps to build up trust, and it shows them that I care and am looking out for them and their careers.

There's no single ratio of "their" vs. "your" talking points to aim for in a one-on-one agenda, nor should there be a target number of items to discuss. Some days there might be just one topic, and others there might be twenty. Being too rigid in format will add unnecessary constraints to the discussion, and make the most important meetings of your week a tad more formal than they need to be. Creating a looser structure means that no topic is off-limits, and you'll be more likely to hear about all the things that are on their mind that should be talked about.

The Importance of a Shared Meeting Agenda

We already talked about how meeting agendas are vital to hosting successful meetings, and one-on-ones are no different. One-on-ones without preplanned agendas are still useful, but they'll be far less effective over time than those that do have them.

One-on-one agendas should be documents shared with both parties, in an easy-to-find and consistent location, and contain all of the historical notes so that all of the context of your previous discussions is in one spot. It should be easy for the direct report to add agenda items to the upcoming meeting without needing to wait on their manager to share something with them too. I use Fellow for my one-on-ones, which does all of the above but also keeps all of the feedback we've exchanged and any goals that are set within the same context as the agenda, while also suggesting various discussion items.

Whatever system you use, the key to a successful one-on-one agenda is that it be prepared ahead of time, and *shared ahead of time* with each other too. By doing that, you'll benefit from the following:

- **You can show up better prepared:** For example, if someone writes a question they have about a specific policy that you don't know the answer to, you can go find the answer before you meet and go over it during the meeting together instead of needing to follow up with them later in a separate conversation.

- **It helps with time keeping:** By knowing what topics there are to discuss, it's easier to figure out how much time you have for each one, and know when it's time to move on to the next one.

Having a shared agenda also means that you have a spot for shared notes to be taken during the one-on-one. Not absolutely every detail of your conversation should be written down, but at a high level anything that involves answers to questions, promises made, and key details should be noted down. It's easy in the moment to think that you'll both be able to remember the conversation, but when you have multiple direct reports and many one-on-ones throughout the year, those finer points will fade in memory. Having them written down means that you can hold each other accountable, and you have something to look back on when you're seeing how your team members have grown and what they've accomplished.

After going through dozens of iterations of one-on-one note templates with various headers meant to solicit a variety of talking points, I've landed on a simple one that doesn't dictate what the conversation should look like, shown as follows.

ONE-ON-ONE MEETING TEMPLATE

Talking Points

- *All discussion topics go here*

What's something you did in the last two weeks that I probably don't know about?

- *Not necessarily talked about during the meeting*

Notepad

- *Any notes during the meeting not specific to discussion topics go here*

All discussion topics go under the *"Talking Points"* header, which is very generically named so that absolutely any topic will fit into it. The only purposefully named section that I include is the second one, *"What's something you did in the last two weeks that I probably don't know about?".* The items listed under that header aren't necessarily talked about aloud in the call, but they're important! When working remotely, a lot of the work that people do is "hidden" in messages and calls that you don't necessarily have access to. I noticed that there were many things that my team members were doing that were incredible, but I wasn't finding out about them until the peer review portion of our feedback cycles—all because we're in general too humble to "brag" about what we've done to our managers. It's important for managers to know about all the really great things that their teams are doing because it helps with feedback and promotions, and it lets you find other opportunities for them to excel in. To make sure that I'm not missing out on these, I have this section in all of my one-on-one templates for each of my team members to write in throughout the week so that they can brag about how incredible they are, guilt-free, because I *want* them to.

Feel free to use this template as a base for your one-on-ones too, and add in any headers to guide the discussions toward topics that are important for your team. Having headers set in your one-on-one template is different than discussion topics that you might add, because when they're present in each one-on-one they start to reinforce what the direct report should be thinking about throughout the week. For example, you could include a header "*What can I help you with this week?*".

Types of One-on-Ones

Most of your one-on-ones will be with your direct reports, and the topics will be whatever you've both added to the agenda based on the events of the week and what's coming up. Every once in a while, there's a need to pivot the one-on-one away from the typical structure and use the meeting for a specific purpose. And sometimes, they aren't even with your direct reports. Here's an overview of different types of one-on-ones and how they differ from what we've already talked about.

The First One-on-One

In Chapter 2, one-on-ones were briefly mentioned as meetings that should be set up in a new hire's first week, on a biweekly cadence. That very first one-on-one that you hold with someone on your team, whether they're new to the company or you're just introducing one-on-ones to a team that is already established, requires a different structure than normal.

While regular one-on-ones are very free-form, the *first* one-on-ones should always be set up with questions and discussion topics that uncover important aspects of each other's working habits and preferences so that you start off on the right foot, and better understand how to work together. Among other questions, I like to ask the following:

- What do you like to do outside of work?

- What motivates you the most?

- What can I do to be the most helpful to you?

- How do you prefer to receive feedback? Slack, email, video call, recorded message, in one-on-ones, ...?

- Is there anything about the team or company that you're confused about, and have felt silly about asking someone about it?

We'll also talk about their and my expectations for the role, what their first few days are looking like, and go over all of the questions that they have for me. This is a very involved version of a one-on-one that revolves mostly around providing context and building the foundations of your relationship. It also sets the tone for how you expect all future one-on-ones to be held! Creating an agenda ahead of time (and making them aware of where they can find it), taking notes of what they're saying, and asking them a lot of questions will set the stage for all future one-on-ones and start the series off on the right foot.

The Feedback One-on-One

Feedback should be exchanged regularly between managers and their team members, going both ways. But more often than not—and largely because of the power imbalance—the feedback being given in one-on-ones is from the manager to the report. Little bits of feedback (both positive and constructive) can always be added to the agenda, but sometimes there are larger items to be discussed, for example, if there's a major issue that needs addressing, or in the more likely case, if you're going over the results of a feedback cycle together.

Regardless of the nature of the feedback being given, if it's a larger item that will need time to be discussed and might cause an emotional reaction, it should take up the majority of the space on the agenda—possibly the entire thing. At Fellow, we run twice-yearly feedback cycles where we collect peer, manager, and direct report feedback on every employee. Because we have this predictable cadence and deadlines for filling out the feedback, I'm able to know with certainty when I'll be ready to provide the summary of the feedback to my team members, which allows me to add it as a discussion item to the agenda well ahead of time so that it doesn't get filled up with too many other topics. I like to use the regularly scheduled one-on-one time to deliver feedback instead of scheduling an entirely separate session to do so, because it makes it feel more routine. We always meet at the same time to discuss our normal one-on-one topics, and so having those discussions during the same time gives it a familiar feel and turns it into more of a variation of our normal discussions rather than a "feedback meeting" that can feel a tad imposing.

The benefits of working that feedback into your one-on-ones include less scheduling overhead to fit twice as many one-on-one-type meetings into a single week as normal, and creating a better atmosphere in which to have those conversations because of the familiarity. Bringing feedback like that into the one-on-one space also makes it easier to bring future feedback up in them too, since there's precedence.

After talking through feedback verbally, I always write out a summary of it (including any agreed-upon actions to come out of it) in the note. This acts as a historical record of our conversation, but more importantly makes it available for the person to read back on later to absorb the feedback in a different format. This can be helpful for better understanding what was said, or act as a reminder if what was verbally communicated was forgotten (it's less awkward than asking your manager for the feedback again!).

The Social One-on-One

Many one-on-one guides will talk about how these meetings absolutely *must* be planned out properly and include a variety of elements (like feedback and coaching) to be useful, every time. While I believe that one-on-ones should be prepared for, and that there should be a general sense of some sort of structure that encourages certain topics to be brought up, I'm strongly against the notion that they need to be useful and directed at work topics *every single time*.

The majority of the time, yes, one-on-ones should be directed in large part toward work-related topics. But not every time! There's a lot of value in the "social" one-on-ones—that is, the one-on-ones that are spent talking about what's going on in life, personal updates, and plans for the weekend. These aren't one-on-ones that are specifically planned out to be this way, they just happen. Often, the social one-on-ones happen when you're working very closely throughout the week with your direct report to the point where you're aware of everything that's going on, and have already had discussions around it all. It's perfectly fine to have weeks like that, where there's just nothing else work related that either of you feel the need to talk about in that dedicated time slot. But even in those cases, it's best not to cancel the one-on-one! A lack of topics on the agenda doesn't mean that there wasn't anything they wanted to talk with you about, and spending time specifically catching up on the social aspect of life helps to strengthen your relationship. These types of one-on-ones have a special place in the world of remote work in particular.

The Peer One-on-One

While the typical "one-on-one" involves a manager and their direct report, it's common to also have "peer one-on-ones." Peer one-on-ones have a different purpose than ones with your team members, but they have similar goals: you might not be coaching each other and delegating opportunities, but you will be exchanging feedback, discussing issues, and building trust with each other.

As a manager, you likely have many peers. There are all of the other engineering managers that report to the same manager as you do, but also all of the cross-functional people that you work with often. For me, that means design, product, sales, marketing, and customer success managers and leaders, in addition to the other engineering managers. Our ability to collectively work together productively is essential for the business, and so I meet with many of them in one-on-ones every few weeks. On top of the many topics specific to whatever we're working on in the moment, and feedback for each other, we talk about topics like

- How are our teams working together? What's going well? What's not going well?

- What do you think is missing from the upcoming roadmap?

- How could we collaborate better?

- What important topics are coming up in the business that we should start talking about?

Having these peer one-on-ones is also a great place to have conversations around how you're feeling as a manager at the moment. There are always going to be tough moments in the role—people leaving, projects going south—things where you can't necessarily express how you truly feel to your team. Having peers that you talk with on a recurring basis gives you that space to express what's going on, and hopefully get input from them. Your peers at work are an important part of your support network in your role.

The Manager One-on-One

In addition to all of the one-on-ones you'll be having where *you're* the manager, you'll also be continuing to have one-on-ones with your own manager. I *love* my one-on-ones with my manager; they're my favorite meeting of the week. Just like peer one-on-ones, one-on-ones with your manager can play the role of being a part of that support network in your role. I like to bring topics every week that I want help with troubleshooting (whether it's interpersonal issues on my team or planning out how we're going to run the next hackathon), and I have the space to freely talk through how I'm feeling about how everything is going—something that I don't necessarily want to do quite as openly with anyone else.

Regardless of where you are in your management journey though, having those scheduled one-on-ones with your manager is just as important as every other one-on-one that you have. Even the most experienced manager can benefit from the coaching, feedback, alignment, and open space to talk that these meetings offer. And just like how one-on-ones with your team are valuable to you, these meetings are valuable to your manager too—after all, you're the link between them and your team, and without strong communication between the two of you, it can isolate an entire group of people from them.

Troubleshooting and Mistakes

One-on-ones aren't the easiest of meetings to run. You can't just step through the agenda and end the call like in any other meeting, they're far more personal than that. They're also the type of meeting that you want to ensure is working really well, for the health of the team and happiness of each member.

The following are a series of common issues around one-on-ones that can mean that they're veering off track, and how to steer them back onto the right path.

When There's "Nothing to Talk About"

Sometimes, people can feel reluctant to host one-on-ones at all because there's often "nothing to talk about," and the meeting ends early because the silence is awkward. This is a symptom of a few potential issues:

- **The purpose of one-on-ones hasn't been communicated clearly to the direct report:** This is a very common issue, and one that I fell into when I first started having these meetings with my manager too! The very first one-on-one you have with each member of your team is a good place to set expectations for what this time should be used for, and how you expect them to prepare. It can be helpful to provide them with samples of what a good agenda might look like and resources with suggestions on how to make the most of the time.[1]

- **The one-on-ones are too frequent:** One-on-ones should take place ideally once per week, but depending on the frequency of your other interactions and what they're working on at the time, it can make sense to change to a biweekly cadence. When you meet less frequently, there are more topics to go over in the one-on-one, making them each more useful.

- **There's no shared agenda being created ahead of time:** When you don't put thought into what you want to discuss with your manager, it's all too easy to go into the call, talk about what you did over the

---

[1] An example of a comprehensive guide to one-on-ones from the direct reports' perspective is this ebook: "The Art of Meeting with Your Manager," https://fellow.app/resources/the-art-of-meeting-with-your-manager/

weekend, and think that there's nothing else that really
needs discussing work-wise, and end the call early.
And instead, you'll end up remembering little things
throughout the week and having entirely separate
conversations instead of bundling them all together
into the one-on-one, which isn't the most efficient use
of everyone's time. Having a shared agenda that's set up
early means that topics can be added to it throughout
the week as you think of them, so that by the time
the one-on-one actually happens, there is a list of
discussion points to go over.

When all else fails and there's nothing that my direct report wants
to talk about in our one-on-one—and we're done with the social catch-
up—I ask a lot of questions. There is *always* something to ask about and
feedback that can be collected. Whether it's asking something as generic
as "What do you think the company could be doing differently," or "What
projects do you want to work on next month," there's an infinite number
of open-ended questions that can be asked. I love asking these types of
questions because they provide so many insights that typically wouldn't
come up otherwise, and they're a terrific view into how people see the
organization. Even if asking someone what they think the company
could be doing differently isn't a time-sensitive agenda topic that would
normally be brought up as an important item, the answers given help you
understand their viewpoints, and often give ideas on how to improve many
aspects of the team.

"We'll Talk As Needed"

This particular issue is more common with people who have had at least
one other manager before and either didn't have one-on-ones at all or
had very unproductive ones that left a sour taste. When faced with the

thought of having one-on-ones with their new manager (you), they might be against the idea and prefer to talk on an as-needed basis instead of in scheduled, recurring meetings.

It might be tempting to think "Yes, works for me, one less meeting per week!". But that would be a mistake! If you don't have regular one-on-ones, when will you go over career goals together, or ask questions about various non-urgent but important topics? Those typical managerial conversations will be far less likely to happen without explicitly scheduled time, which isn't good for the direct report's career growth. Having the scheduled one-on-ones also protects your time: instead of having multiple small interruptions throughout the week to discuss things as needed, they can be bundled together in one dedicated time slot.

Fixing this issue takes time, because it usually requires rebuilding the person's idea of what a one-on-one is, and showing them how useful it can be. Steps to get there include *making sure the one-on-ones happen*, sharing resources explaining what good one-on-ones look like, and always bringing a few of your own agenda items to the meeting so that there's always something to talk about.

The Emotional Overload

One-on-ones are often the medium through which your team will share bad news with you, and sensitive topics might be brought up. Someone might tell you about something really difficult that's happening in their personal lives, or they might talk about how they're being impacted by an event that's taken place in the world—whatever it is, it's likely to happen at least a few times throughout your time as a manager.

There are two parts to these types of conversations that make them so difficult:

- You need to react properly in the moment, and provide the appropriate level of support/accommodations for them at work.

- You need to protect your own mental wellbeing when having to deal with the emotional weight of all the adversity that each of your reports might be facing.

On the first point, to summarize Lara Hogan's article "Managing in Terrible Times"[2] (which I recommend reading in full), focus on how your direct report is feeling and what you can do to support them, rather than redirecting the conversation to how you're feeling about it with statements like "It makes me feel sad that this is happening to you," which can lead to *them* feeling the need to comfort *you*.

On the second point, as a manager, you'll hear about many of the highs and lows in the lives of each member of your team. It's so exciting to get to celebrate the highs with them, but the lows can add up quickly, especially if there are multiple people going through tough times at once. And since you're a manager, you probably have a lot of empathy for people, which means that those sad feelings will hit extra hard.

I've gone through times where bad news was shared with me in nearly every one-on-one in a week, things totally beyond anyone's control. It's easy to feel helpless in those situations because as much as you can try to make work life easier for them, there's nothing that you can do to make the problem go away entirely. After those conversations in particularly hard weeks when the emotional load gets to be too much, I'll collapse onto the couch and need time to recover—especially in situations where I'll have one bad news–filled one-on-one followed by a very happy one, where

---

[2] https://larahogan.me/blog/being-a-manager-in-terrible-times/

there's a lot of emotional whiplash. That's another benefit of having one-on-ones remotely: you can better mask that state (which something that I would normally not recommend doing with your team, but news shared in one-on-ones should be treated as confidential, and showing strong emotions to others after having those conversations betrays a bit of that).

This is the one troubleshooting issue that I have no clear-cut solution for, just advice: feeling this way is completely normal (you are not alone if it's the case), and *you are not responsible for fixing everything that's going wrong in your team's lives.* You can be there to listen and support them, and make changes at work if needed to accommodate them, but *nobody* is expecting you to solve the core issues. It can be difficult to truly absorb that because a lot of your job involves solving issues for them at work, and this is possibly *affecting* work, but it is not up to you.

Takeaways from This Chapter

- One-on-ones might be the only time that an engineer gets to spend time alone with their manager and bring up topics that might not be appropriate in larger group meetings, and it gives them the opportunity to have time and thought dedicated to whatever it is that they want to talk about.

- An employee's happiness at their job is in large part dictated by their relationship with their manager. One-on-ones are the best tool at your disposal for building and maintaining that bond and trust with each member on your team.

- One-on-ones when remote are extremely important, because they might be the one time per week that you get to speak with each of your reports individually.

- Remote one-on-ones are even better than in-person ones because you can choose a private location for sensitive discussions.

- It's okay to play around with the schedule of one-on-ones over time to find something that works for you and your team. The important aspects to consider are the length, day of the week, time of day, and frequency. Start with 30 minutes biweekly on a Tuesday, Wednesday, or Thursday, and adjust as necessary from there.

- One-on-ones should almost never be cancelled or moved.

- Share the task of preparing for one-on-ones with your reports; the burden of creating the agenda shouldn't be entirely on them. Preparing for these meetings shows that you care about their careers.

- Having a written, collaborative, and preplanned agenda for your one-on-ones is critical.

- Being too rigid in the agenda format will add unnecessary constraints to the discussion, and make the most important meetings of your week a tad more formal than they need to be. Creating a looser structure means that no topic is off-limits, and you'll be more likely to hear about all the things that are on their mind that should be talked about.

- It's okay to not have anything other than social updates to talk about once in a while.

- Schedule one-on-ones with your peers, where you can talk through issues you're each facing, and exchange feedback about how your teams are working together. Your relationship will have a large impact on how your teams work together too.

- Being a manager means that you're likely going to hear about a lot of bad things that are going on in your team members' lives. That adds up, and it's really hard. Take breaks as needed to not get emotionally overwhelmed, and remember that your job is not to solve everything that they're facing in life.

CHAPTER 5

Deploys

Code deploys are among the most common and process-oriented tasks that an engineer will take on. Long gone are the days where most software is distributed on physical CDs and needs to be in near-perfect condition because of the incredible cost to shipping (literally) corrections. Nowadays when you work in tech, you're likely working in a SaaS environment where the product is some form of web-based application and updates can go out at any moment—even if you're working on software for hardware-based products like cars, watches, thermostats, or fridges, these devices are all internet connected, and the burden of updating them is so minor compared to the undertaking that it was before.

Being able to ship updates so quickly has changed the way that the development of software happens in general, from planning requirements all the way to deploying it. Since it's so easy to push out updates, the quality bar for initial versions of products isn't quite as high as it would have been before (when fixing bugs would have been extremely costly and meant starting up an entire supply chain to send out more CDs). While one clear direct benefit of this to engineers is that not every single edge case needs to be accounted for, there is an even larger implication that affects the product and its development at a fundamental level. Instead of deciding up front what the entire product should encompass, it's possible to iterate on features, run experiments, and make data-driven decisions that shape features while continuously making the product better for all. Being able to deploy changes to code often is a great benefit all around!

A. Sunderland, *Remote Engineering Management*,
https://doi.org/10.1007/978-1-4842-8584-8_5

And now, it's something that many teams are doing at least multiple times per week, possibly multiple times per day (or maybe even multiple times per minute within large companies).

It's hopefully something that is highly process oriented and either happens automatically when some code has passed all required automated tests or happens very easily when someone just presses a button. Hopefully, you aren't manually SSHing into a server and manually pulling the latest changes from git and restarting services—but if you are, I hope that it's at least highly documented (and that you work toward getting a better system in place soon, for your engineers' and your own sake).

But we aren't going to actually talk about how to best do deploys from a technical perspective, because that depends heavily on the team, the type of code they're writing, and their delivery cadence, among other factors. Instead, what I'm going to be describing in this chapter is a topic that's common to all deploy types—no matter their setup: how all the people in and around the process *feel*. Because yes, even this very process-heavy and sometimes automatic task that takes place so often involves a lot of emotions. And chaos! And as we talked about before, understanding the emotional state of the team is hard when you're working remotely because it's easy to mask feelings behind the screen and portray oneself in a different light during video calls throughout the day.

Before getting to the emotional chaos of deploying code, we're going to cover something more concrete: how to plan and organize deploys while remote. This is for those times where something big is being launched: a large project that involves a lot of new code and database migrations, probably a big addition to the user interface, and a lot of people—because these types of launches can become a communication nightmare where everything is siloed.

Getting Everyone on the Same Page

For the purpose of illustration, we're going to assume that this deploy revolves around the launch of a major project which involves multiple team members, and is for a SaaS-based product—something where there are multiple other non-engineering teams as stakeholders, such as customer success, marketing, or sales. If the team has reached the stage where the product is ready to launch, it's likely that the communication of status updates for the projects themselves has been going well throughout their lifecycle (see Chapter 6 on communication strategies for tips on managing status updates while remote), and now what is being dealt with is the communication around updates for the specifics of the deploy itself.

The first two things that you have to do to set the team up for success are to designate someone as the DRI (Directly Responsible Individual) for the deploy, and create a note where everyone can throw any information that is relevant or to-dos so that everyone can be aware without needing to follow a dozen Slack channels and keep up with the multitude of discussions that are likely ongoing throughout and leading up to this process. The person responsible for coordinating the deploy might be you, but should be someone with strong communication skills and at least basic knowledge of what is going out and who is responsible for each part—typically a manager, or an engineer with seniority. They aren't necessarily responsible for actually getting the code out there or doing any of the changes themselves, but they are responsible for making sure that everyone does what they need to and that each team is communicating with each other and bringing up any blockers, issues, or dependencies. Having a single person in this position makes things go more smoothly.

The note that is set up should exist at least 24–48 hours before the deploy happens, and should include some basic headers to categorize information: "*To do before deploy*," "*To do after deploy*," "*To test after deploy*," and "*Info*," for example. This should be made available to all engineers who are even tangentially involved in the process, so that they can add anything that they're nervous about and things that absolutely should be tested once they hit production (of course, they'd be tested ahead of time too, but may need reverification on production because of a different environment setup). This gives everyone a good idea as to what needs to happen before the deploy goes live (maybe flipping a switch, setting up a URL route, etc.), and what needs to happen immediately after the deploy before everyone can celebrate. The "Info" section can include anything that anyone thinks is relevant—for example, if it's expected that there'll be a burst of new tasks running immediately after the deploy, which would normally look out of the ordinary, that's something the team responsible might want to write down so that the other teams don't worry and think that something is going wrong when they see that.

Adding to this note should be actively encouraged by managers and team leads. It's the type of thing that's immensely useful when everyone is working on it, but takes a bit of getting used to before it's normal to write down all the necessary information. On our team, we use Fellow for this. We have a shared "Product & Engineering" Google Calendar set up with important dates for the build cycles and events for large deploys that we do. Then it's just a matter of opening up the note for that event in Fellow, applying the template with those headers that we've saved, and we're good to go—no need for anyone to set up the document or remember to share it out beforehand. While you're doing the deploy, keep that note open and check things off as you go. It's good to use it almost like a launch checklist, and it makes the Directly Responsible Individual's job a tad easier too because they don't have to remember all the information collected from different teams, or create this note themselves.

Managing the Emotional Chaos of Deploys

You may be wondering, since when is deploying code emotional? It's so process filled, how is there any space for feelings? There are many emotions going on around deploys, and not just from people who are nervous in general about how it'll pan out, or worried when things go wrong—and also, not only from just developers, a lot of people are involved in this. While there might be some easy-to-spot emotions like the feelings of fear and dread when the servers are on fire (which I'm sure we've probably all been through and understand the gist of them—I've certainly had my fair share of incidents to manage), we're going to focus on the hidden ones that might not be so easy to spot.

Throughout the rest of this chapter are a series of scenarios to do with various aspects of deploys where people might have particularly strong emotional reactions, and how to adapt the situation to account for and hopefully lessen them. It's not possible to entirely neutralize the emotions that we'll talk about, nor should that be the goal. While we want people to feel at ease on the team overall and not be filled with too much doubt or confusion, a smidge of nerves keeps people on their toes. Being a tad nervous about a major deploy means that you're more likely to triple-check the work and catch issues ahead of time, instead of overconfidently relying on other people and systems. Our focus as engineering managers should then be to remove the aspects around deploys that cause negatively impacting emotions (those that hurt our performance or sense of belonging), without creating too large and soft of a safety net that removes the emotions that drive us to do better.

The New Team Member

Situation

There's a new person on the team, and their code is going live for the first time ever at the company, hooray!

Since they haven't participated in a deploy here yet, they're not entirely sure what the process is like. They're nervous that they possibly haven't tested it enough, because they know they aren't familiar with every single aspect of the project yet. This is common even with senior engineers who have done plenty of deploys in their career. Going through this process for the first time in a new environment with unfamiliar systems, people, and processes is nerve-wracking!

Solution

A large portion of the fears here can be minimized by maintaining team documentation around deploys (this goes back to the "team documentation" from Chapter 2). This documentation should explain the mechanics of a deploy such as when they happen, who does them, whether they're automatic, how they work behind the scene, and what to do when something goes wrong. Having all of this information written down helps to more easily scale the team size, because people can learn from it instead of asking basic questions and being walked through it individually.

For this particular scenario, it also acts as a good point of reassurance because the new hire will have a stronger understanding of what is going to be happening when their code goes live, creating a more predictable and stable environment which feels safer. As a manager, outside of this documentation for the first deploy, it's important to also talk through their code changes with them, and congratulate them when it's live!

The QA Analyst's Bug Reports
Situation

A member of the QA team has created a list of bugs in the new features that are going out in the deploy, and has reported them to the engineering team that built them. The engineers, stressed and trying to get everything built as quickly as possible, push back saying that the bugs aren't important, and that they can fix them in a later release. This causes the (equally stressed) QA analyst to feel like their work isn't being recognized and seen as important, because their role in this deploy is to find and report issues while making sure that they get fixed before going live.

Their personal feeling of success is measured on the quality and bugless experience of the product in the production environment, and in this situation the engineers are actively harming that success. It can feel as though the engineers don't believe that their work matters. Ultimately, it's up to the developers to actually fix the bugs and make sure that the work to be done is addressed, which can make them feel even more powerless over the situation. This isn't a good spot to be putting the QA analysts in!

Solution

When the deploy date is coming up quickly, it's important for both QA and engineering to be on the same page as the product team about what types of issues are acceptable, what the fault tolerance is, and what paths need to be flawless before launching.

For example, everyone might agree that authentication needs to be functional with an extremely low failure rate, but that it's okay if the somewhat hidden and unused data export button sometimes breaks when there are over 10,000,000 rows in the CSV, which would only affect one in a million users—that can be fixed later. Having that alignment ahead of time on what is most important (and what's not) makes issue prioritization easier for the QA team, and better aligns them with the engineering team on the goals. This makes communication more efficient (there's less back and forth about whether a given issue is important), and everyone is much less likely to be upset about a decision that another team makes, because everyone has that shared context.

The Rush for Last-Minute Code

Situation

When a date has been set for a deploy, it can cause a bit of panic. Let's be honest, it's extremely rare that all of the code that's meant to go out by a release date is 100% written and in perfect condition, with every single potential feature that was pitched being included in it. It's far more likely that there are a handful of non-blocking bugs that are still being fixed, a team is still finishing up a critical path because we totally forgot about this one thing, and someone is done with the MVP version of their feature and is now trying to speed-write some code to quickly fit in one last bonus feature in time for the code to go live. I've been guilty of this far too many times before.

It's so easy to fall into the trap of thinking that we can absolutely get this "simple" thing out in the next few hours and ready to go live with everything else, making the product team and customers beaming with joy. But our eyes are bigger than our mouths, and usually the bit of code that we thought would take just an hour ends up taking a little longer. There are no tests, we skip over a few best practices, and don't fully run through it locally before pushing to the repository (because if you can't see a bug, it hopefully doesn't exist). It gets merged without too much code review because everyone else is also busy getting everything ready, and then the QA team may or may not even have time to test it out before it goes live. And then if it makes it onto production, either you're extremely lucky and everything works out just perfectly—or you're not, and the support tickets start rolling in, the bug reports and logs start piling up, and you're in another (more urgent) race against the clock to fix the code that you now can't quite roll back because it doesn't look good to take features away from people once they're out there.

Being in this situation causes a slew of emotions for so many people: for the engineers who feel rushed, exhilarated, and then deflated; for the QA team who feels taken advantage of for not having the proper time to do their job; for the product team who is excited that the launch will go a little above and beyond what was promised, only for that "above and beyond" to turn negative; and for the support team, who probably didn't have much of a heads-up about this last-minute thing going live, and now has to deal with all the inquiries and angry customers writing in about it not working.

Solution

This is something that can be harder to catch while remote, because you can't actively see that someone is working on something past what's expected of them by just passing by their desk—it's something that you may not even notice until the deploy is actually complete. But there is a way to help prevent it! Of course, this is still bound to happen once in a while—we're all a little overambitious sometimes.

Something that we do at Fellow when we're planning large or complex releases is to institute a "code freeze." This is where you determine a date and time after which point only bug fixes can be merged into the release branch; no new features or add-ons will be allowed after that. While this can be officially mandated with controls on merge access for the repositories where the code is kept, in most cases it's best to avoid putting those hard controls in place and instead trusting the team and telling them that you trust their judgment and that you expect them to maintain a high quality of release. Placing this trust in them and making it explicit makes this whole situation much less likely: instead of rushing to beat an automated system to get their code in before they're locked out, they now want to maintain the trust that you have in them, and don't want to do something to break that (or the build). Putting the onus of the quality of the release on them also gives them even more ownership over their code, and they'll be less likely to merge code that they're unsure of because they know that it will be looked on as their mistake if something breaks, and not something that they can easily pass off as being "QA's mistake" for not finding the bugs before it went live.

A few days before this, it's also important for the product and engineering teams to have a mutual understanding of how far along the feature is, and which parts are possibly not going to make it into the release. The goals set should be realistic, and as long as they are, there shouldn't be a need to be quickly writing last-minute code to get this "one last thing" in.

Forgetting About Time Zones
Situation

When deploying a large project, it's common to block off a bit of time during a period of low traffic so that as few people as possible are affected if anything goes wrong. For a lot of internet-based SaaS businesses, there are potentially *no* low traffic times, because anyone around the world can be using the service at any point. For many though, these peaks and valleys of usage still exist, maybe because you haven't been available in the market in another continent yet, or maybe because the nature of the product is time specific (e.g., stock market software). But also by nature of being a remote company, you may have team members who work across different time zones.

When you're choosing a time to deploy code as a team, it's important to take into account who needs to be present for the deploy (if anyone), and what time it will be in their time zones (or whether it's significantly outside of their normal work schedule). When a time is set for the deploy but there's no communication around who needs to be present (or there is, but there's no thought put into what time it is for that person), it can feel isolating.

Solution

Even if 4:00am in someone's time zone is the only possible time for the deploy (at which point you may want to pause and evaluate why that is), communicating to them that you recognize that it's that time for them and understand that it's not ideal shows them that you took them into account and are not just passing over them as another "resource" to get things done on the team. They're a real person with real lives—and real sleep needs! As much as possible, everyone's time zone should be taken into account, but at the very least it should be communicated with everyone that you're aware of the situation so that they know their needs and time matter.

Tip   Even if every member of your team is working within the same time zone, normalize including the time zone in any times that you communicate with them. Even with the small act of specifying that you'll be away until "2pm ET" in a Slack message to the team, you're demonstrating that you're aware you aren't the center of work. And, getting into this habit means that when the timing is really important (like for deploys), you'll be less likely to forget about what a chosen time means for those in other time zones.

Should I Stay or Should I Go?
Situation

Related to the previous section: regardless of time zones, make sure that everyone is aware of whether they personally need to be present for the deploy! If you're deploying all the code late at night and you haven't explicitly defined who the key people that need to stick around in case of issues are, it's more likely than not that you'll end up with a lot of engineers sitting by their work computers late at night, watching the communication

113

channels and waiting to see if anything comes up that they need to do. This uncertainness of whether they're needed causes a disruption to their lives, and can cause fear that they're forgetting to do something that they're supposed to know about.

Solution

This is especially the case with people who have contributed smaller features to large deploys, or people who are still new to the team— especially if you don't have that team-based deploy documentation letting them know how the deploy is going to go down. Well ahead of the deploy, work with the teams to compile a list of the people who must be present for the deploy, and make sure that everyone is aware of who is required to be virtually present, who must be reachable in case of emergency, and who does not need to be around. This is not telling people that they aren't important, it's telling people that you value their time and want to make sure that they aren't being taken advantage of. Being able to tell them this well ahead of time ensures that those whose presence isn't required won't be unnecessarily cancelling plans in order to sit at home and stare at their screens. And for those people who are required to be present, if it's after hours for them, make sure that they're getting properly compensated for that time, or get to take that equivalent time off within the next few days to make up for the disruption.

The Day After

Situation

The deploy isn't over when the code is live and everything is up and running! There is still a lot of impact that it can have the next day on all of the other teams in the organization, outside of engineering. And if the communication between departments wasn't structured properly ahead of time, there can be chaos with teams such as sales and customer support.

Sales team members can have dozens of meetings with potential clients scheduled every week, and that means that they have their demo memorized down to the last click. They may have a few variants, and there will be a few paths they could go down here and there, but it's by and large the same demo that they give day after day. It allows them to be efficient, and reduces the likelihood that they'll make mistakes; it's also something that's been tested over many iterations, and adapted over time to be the most effective as possible at conveying the right points and selling people on whatever it is they're selling. They could recite it backward and forward in their sleep. So when deploys take place that change the user interface even in the slightest, possibly something like moving a button from a top-level menu into a submenu—or worse, a major interface overhaul—it understandably throws them off. And in the worst case, they might discover this change while they're in their first demo of the day! This can cause panic and make the difference between a sale or no sale: people are less likely to buy software that even the supposed "experts" are getting confused by, or which changes unpredictably.

Customer support teams are in charge of writing help center documentation for customers, replying to emails and in-product chat messages when people have questions or encounter issues, running virtual meetings where they walk through solutions, and even answering phone calls to help clients out. They have an enormous amount of knowledge on the ins and outs of how the product they work with functions, and are able to spot patterns that may point to larger system failures when tracking trends across incoming inquiries.

One of their key success metrics is often the "time to resolution": the total time elapsed between when someone first reaches out and submits an inquiry about a particular issue and the time that they're able to resolve it to the person's satisfaction. This time to resolution metric can be a measure of the team's success and effectiveness, and can even be used in determining whether they will be getting their bonus paid out in full or not. It's a big deal! So any kind of disruption to that metric can rightfully make the team upset, especially when the disruption is out of their control. Issues that arise after deploys (whether it's bugs or general confusion over a new interface) can be a major detractor for this number's success, especially if the team hasn't yet been properly brought up to speed on the new changes that went live (let alone write help center documentation about it): it will take them more time than normal to answer, because they need to go learn the answers for themselves too. This can easily cause the team to feel uncertain with the potential for this same unpredictable change to happen in the future, and upset with the engineers, who wrote the code that had the bugs and are otherwise unaffected by the position that the support team is in.

Solution

The solution to both of these situations is to set up strong communication practices across all relevant departments early, and be in constant communication. Both situations could be avoided if everyone was made aware well in advance about what changes would be going live, giving them enough time to adjust their demos, write help center documentation, and understand the implications of the features and how to explain them to users.

There are a few strategies that I've seen work for this. One method is to make use of asynchronous communication since we're in a remote environment. On my team, we like to record videos explaining the features and doing deep dives into all the moving parts, and send those to the managers of each relevant team so they can distribute to the people on their teams that would benefit from watching them. These demos are sometimes done in conjunction with the product team too, when they're particularly complicated and require an in-depth business explanation. Having a recorded video means that it's easy to refer back to, rewind, speed up, or skip around, because every team will have different needs and this allows them to adapt it to what they need—without needing to have live demos multiple times for each team.

A good addition to the recorded video strategy is to also host synchronous informational meetings. These are meetings where the team leads, managers, or any critical stakeholder for a project will come together on a regular recurring basis and discuss topics such as upcoming features, insights from sales, marketing requirements, and other ideas or concerns. This is a great time for everyone to learn from each other, and properly plan out releases from start to finish while including all stakeholder teams.

The cadence of this meeting will depend on the release cadence for the teams involved, but a good place to start is once every two weeks, for 50 minutes. Set agenda headers in a shared meeting note to prompt people to add all or the information listed earlier as discussion items (e.g., a header could be *"Cross-functional tasks and asks"*). Be on the lookout for the meeting growing to be too large (where not everyone gets the chance to speak anymore), or growing too much in scope. Ideally, all of the conversations will stay relevant to the majority of teams represented, and any sidebars (e.g., the sales team coordinating with the marketing team about something that doesn't need to include the design and engineering teams) can happen at a later point, to be conscious of everyone's time. This is a highly collaborative meeting that is best run synchronously (i.e., over a call). It typically involves a lot of discussion, and it's easier for everyone to collaborate on those discussions in real time. However, all of the preparation for the meeting can still be done asynchronously—having a shared agenda allows everyone to inform others of what they'd like to talk about and think through discussion topics ahead of time, possibly even resolving some of them before the meeting officially starts.

Takeaways from This Chapter

- Deploys are very process-heavy events, but also involve a lot of emotions and feelings from all sorts of people even tangentially involved.

- Appoint a Directly Responsible Individual who is in charge of making sure that teams communicate with each other and the deploy gets done. They don't need to know about how every little detail of the things going out works, but should have a high-level overview so that they know who to reach out to.

- Create a shared note between all people who have code going out in the deploy with various headers that make them write out any thoughts they have, any to-do items for before or after the deploy, and things to test. This makes it easier for everyone to stay informed without needing to be directly involved with all projects.

- Write as much documentation as possible around how the deploys work, so that new team members can read through it and feel more comfortable when it's time for their code to go out. And remember to congratulate them when it does!

- Set a common understanding between the engineering, QA, and product teams working on features going out in a release so that when bugs are found, everyone is on the same page as to their importance.

- When a major release is going live, set a "code freeze" date and time after which only bug fixes are allowed to be merged to the release branch. That will help avoid situations where engineers are rushing to write code for "one last little thing" that ends up not being properly written or tested. Explicitly put the trust in the team to release a high-quality feature, and that sense of trust and ownership will make them less likely to rush lower-quality features into the deploy.

- When choosing a time for the deploy, make sure that those in different time zones than your own are aware that you know what time it will be for them, and make sure they know whether their presence is required or not. That acknowledgment that you are thinking about them and their lives goes a long way toward building trust as a team.

- Regardless of time zone, make sure that everyone involved is aware of who needs to be present for the deploy, who needs to be reachable in case of emergency, and who does not need to be present. Allow the required attendees to take the equivalent time spent off in the next few days in case this is outside of normal working hours. Telling someone that their presence is not required for a deploy will not insult and will instead allow them to not sit by their computer all night waiting to see if they're needed, causing a disruption to their lives.

- Communicate early and often with members of non-engineering teams, such as sales and customer support, and provide relevant information so that no one is caught off guard when a release happens which may impact their work.

CHAPTER 6

Communication Strategies

For people who haven't embraced the incredibleness that is remote work yet, one of the biggest concerns that's often brought up as holding them back is the fear that there won't be enough communication between people.

It's a fear that shows an overreliance on old-school management techniques: walking around the office checking in on team members by going up to their desks and interrupting whatever deep state of work they were in to ask how it's going. These are the same companies that will schedule so many meetings, that people can't reasonably get much work done during the day, and rely on random chance encounters "around the water cooler" for new innovations to come about and for teams to properly collaborate. If they were to pivot toward remote work, they'd likely be turning every in-person meeting they had into a virtual one, and maybe even require everyone to sit on camera all day with their teammates—they wouldn't be truly embracing the world of remote work and the many advantages that it brings to both personal and work life.

Working remotely is an entirely different mindset than working in an office. It requires different ways of planning projects, different ways of interacting with work product, and a multitude of new ways of communicating with each other. If you take every meeting you might normally schedule in an office and bring it into the remote workplace,

© Alexandra Sunderland 2022
A. Sunderland, *Remote Engineering Management*,
https://doi.org/10.1007/978-1-4842-8584-8_6

you'll be overwhelming people with video call fatigue, and reducing the amount of concentration and focus that people are able to bring to their work. When you're joining a meeting virtually, people can't see your screen unless you're presenting it, so it's very easy to get away with doing other non-call things on it when you aren't actively participating at the moment (or even if you are). I'm guilty of this too; when I find my focus draining at the end of a long day of back-to-back meetings, I'll start browsing the internet, maybe even playing a quick game or two of 2048 on the side while I passively pay attention to the discussion, just enough so that if someone says my name I could reasonably answer. This isn't a good way of going about structuring work, because it eliminates all the great parts of working remotely. Having too many meetings or other real-time conversations means that people are constricted to their desks at certain times, need to be in an area where it's reasonable to speak out loud (no working in a busy coffee shop), and might need to adjust their work schedule and interrupt their hours of deep-focus work time.

In this chapter, we'll talk about how to move away from the old-school way of thinking about communication; no longer will remote teams need to all be online and on a call all day together, or constantly writing messages back and forth to each other and expecting that real-time communication. Instead, we'll take a different approach to staying informed around things that typically require communication on engineering teams, and talk about different ways of using technology to get the point across.

Staying Updated

One of the big worries of becoming a first-time remote manager of a team is when thinking about how you'll stay up to date with what everyone is working on.

The thought is that if your team were colocated, everyone would be giving regular verbal updates on what they're doing in conversation passively, and it would be easy to stroll by their desk and ask for a status update if required—maybe even just peer over their shoulder to take a peek at their monitor (please don't do this). The truth is, those were never good strategies for staying up to date with people anyway. It may have worked for you as the manager, but how did the product managers, designers, or quality analysts stay up to date? Did they need to pass by those desks too and get their updates in the same way? That's introducing far more interruptions to the engineer's workday than they should be receiving, and every time someone gets an update, it'll be different from the last person's, and they won't benefit from hearing each other's questions. There's a lot that's going on there that's wrong, and makes everyone's job harder; this method of staying updated on the status of work product is not the way to go.

The virtual equivalent of that strategy is for every individual who is working with an engineer on a project to send them a direct message periodically asking what the latest news is. The result here is the same, potentially even *worse* because there's no possibility whatsoever for that siloed written conversation to be overheard and joined in on by others. The solution might sound obvious: schedule a meeting so that all those individual people can get together and have that series of conversations in one go. But that would also be wrong! If we were to schedule a meeting in this situation, we would be back to the bad state that we talked about at the start of this chapter, where the benefits of remote work are not truly being lived, and people starting to get overloaded with meetings (especially as the manager, with multiple engineers on the team and many people to coordinate things with). Instead of doing that, there are some tactics that can be employed to make sure that everyone who needs to be informed is always on the same page, and no one has to reach out for info directly to any of the engineers, who can provide information and updates on their own time.

For the following suggestions, I'm making the assumption that engineers are working on a project together with other non-engineer stakeholders, it lasts multiple weeks, and there will at some point be an end to this project and code will be released somewhere—a fair assumption for the majority of cases. When we're working in a setup like this, as I often am as someone who manages product-focused engineering teams, whenever a project is started we set up right off the bat a few different channels for different types of communication. Each one has a distinct purpose and is best used for different styles of conversation, different types of involvement, and different points in time during the week. No matter what we're working on, we always lean into the communication patterns set out by these best practices. Once the hurdle of creating each channel has been passed, it's easier to work within this system than to work without it. Using these techniques, we almost never have to have unscheduled calls to discuss progress, or end up in a situation where we're lacking information about what's going on. Here is how to structure communication around these types of projects.

Unstructured Written Communication

Every new project that we're working on, no matter how small, gets its own channel (conversation) in Slack. These are always made public internally (not private) so that anyone in the company who wants to can seek them out and join them to catch up on the latest happenings. While we use Slack, any product that offers the same general idea of group-based chat will work here—for example, MS Teams, Discord, or even Google Chat.

Tip   Unless something that truly needs to be kept confidential is being discussed, there's no good reason to keep a project channel private and artificially gatekeep information. This goes for communication around other topics too: unless there's a strong case for it, discussions should be kept "in the open" (as opposed to in private channels or direct message) where anyone internally could access them if they wanted. This helps to keep everyone informed about what's going on, and works toward creating a culture of information transparency.

We prefix the names of all our project channels with "project-" so that it's easy to identify what a channel's purpose is (e.g., the name "project-feedback" implies that you're building something around feedback, but just "feedback" sounds more like you're hoping to receive feedback in that channel). This list can get pretty unwieldy quickly if you have a fast-paced build cycle, so it's good practice to archive the channels after a project has concluded. Archiving—not deleting—makes sure that the content is still available and available to search over, but will clear it out of everyone's conversation lists. This is an important step to keep information overload to a minimum while still keeping a record of decisions made and conversations in case anything needs to be referenced.

Once the channel has been created, set it up by doing the following right off the bat:

- Invite all the relevant people who will be involved in the project, whether they're the ones actively working on it, or those that won't be actively participating but should remain informed about decisions and progress.

- Add a description to it that explains its purpose, so that anyone who stumbles upon it understands what is going on and what the communication in it is about.

- Add all of the relevant links for the project to an easily accessible location within it (pinned messages, linked in the header, etc.). For example, links to design documents, requirement files, pull requests, or tech specs.

125

The purpose of this channel isn't so that there's a space for communication and real-time message collaboration: it's a hub that will be bringing together every other step in this toolkit of communication systems. Many teams coordinate a lot of their work through Slack and other messaging platforms, which means that it's an easy place to put information with a high likelihood that people will actually see it—as opposed to stashing things away in a document somewhere, or being lost in the void of a meeting-note-less call.

This channel shouldn't have too many direct "real-time" discussions in it, only the odd question here and there that is particularly time sensitive or of a blocking nature. Most discussions will be happening in the next two topics we'll cover, and their results will appear within this channel.

Cyclic Written Check-Ins

To make sure that everyone involved in a project is aware of what the current status is and what work is being done (or where things are stuck), we set up a system to prompt people for daily updates. In particular, we have a Slack Workflow[1] set up so that every weekday at a specific time (time zone and work schedule dependent on the person, but typically around 4pm their time), a message is posted in the project channel saying "Hello! How did the project go today? Any updates, blockers, or questions?". Then anyone who has anything to say (including engineers, designers, product managers, QA, and others) will post in the thread of that bot message, adding in text and screenshots with the work they accomplished that day, talk about anything they're stuck on (in a form of rubber duck debugging), and ask any somewhat time-sensitive questions.

---

[1] Slack provides a no-code interface to create your own workflows which are various actions chained together that start when something specific happens. For example, you can create a workflow that sends a message to someone who joins a given channel, or even trigger actions in third-party apps.

This might smell like a virtual stand-up in disguise, every engineer's favorite type of meeting. But the smallest difference, the time of day that it's sent, makes a big difference in how it's perceived. Because it's sent at the end of the day and asks how things went, it doesn't feel like a stand-up anymore. There's no pressure to accomplish the things you're writing down, because you're only writing what you did. That still does help keep people on track because you never want to get to the end of the day and not have anything to write down, but it's a different kind of pressure. The end-of-day update is like a reward for a job well done, while the start-of-day update is a potential future disappointment for not completing the work. There's also no time limit on when you need to post in there by: it's available about an hour before the engineer will typically end their workday so that there's time to write in there (and potentially time to seek out answers if necessary too), but it can be completed at any point after it's posted so that people can read through what's going on the next morning when they're getting caught up.

But best of all, we make these fun. They show up as "Project Chickens" because "check-ins" sounds like chicken. And they have chicken emojis, and a rotating set of chicken images based on a theme we set for the year. Maybe that's all the traditional stand-up meeting is missing to make it loved.

Recurring Meetings

While it's probably *possible* to get away with building out a project without any meetings whatsoever, our teams choose to host them once per week for each project so that we can go deeper with the discussions and cover more ground in a shorter time period because of how much faster the back and forth can be.

We schedule these as weekly for 45 minutes, and set them up as recurring events right from the very start of the project so that we always know exactly when we'll be meeting throughout its lifecycle.

All stakeholders are included right from the start too, including the QA team whose job gets much easier when they have the same context as the engineers do around why something was built the way that it was, and what scopes were cut for the first version, because they've been included in each update and all of the various conversations that took place to make decisions. See Chapter 3 on meetings to understand how to properly schedule this meeting and what aspects need to be considered to make it successful.

The 45-minute length is for multiple reasons: by not making it a full hour long, you're allowing those with back-to-back meetings to have a break between them, and it's an amount of time that's just long enough to get good discussions going, and just short enough that you have to be really conscious of time and focus on making those decisions and moving through the topics without talking in circles. The most important aspect of this meeting, and the one thing that will make or break it, is the presence of an agenda. These types of meetings are so filled to the brim with information and decisions that if there's no common area to write down what needs to be talked about and all the decisions that were made, people will forget or walk away with different ideas of what was discussed, and the project will veer off track quickly. The agenda also needs to be available for everyone to contribute to early on, so that as soon as a question comes up it can be added to the note before it's forgotten, and so that people can read it as it's added and start thinking of their answer to it long before the meeting starts. The presence of that shared agenda is one of the key aspects to keeping the meeting length down, because it's allowing participants to prepare ahead of time for all the discussions. The agenda also ideally has a series of headers within it that guides people on how to think about structuring their discussion points and any topics they may want to bring up. For example, having headers *"Updates," "Blockers,"* and *"Questions"* makes people wonder throughout the week, "Do I have any blockers?", and will get them to proactively add them to the agenda to be solved.

To manage all of this and to keep every weekly note in the same easily accessible spot for historical reference, we at Fellow of course use our own product internally. This allows us to see every week's edition of the meeting in one spot, and we can create and set a template for that specific project meeting which gets applied to all future occurrences of it so that no one has to go through the trouble of setting it up, and it automatically reminds meeting attendees if they haven't yet filled out the required sections in the note with their updates and questions—it takes a lot of the burden of thought and effort away from the project manager! As discussions happen and we have things that we need to do that come out of it, it also lets us track our action items and notifies us when they need follow-up. Overall though, the purpose of this project meeting is to get out of the way all of the long discussions that may take just a few minutes verbally, but could drag on for a while if you're writing back and forth. By getting everyone into the virtual room at the same time, it also allows for everyone to be a part of the conversation instead of just those who happen to see messages in the channel at the right time.

In Summary

Those three methods are the most helpful ways of staying updated on ongoing projects on a remote team that I've experienced. They ensure that no one is getting constantly interrupted because people are pushing out updates rather than being polled for them, and the things that aren't urgent and require a conversation are all discussed at the same predictable time with all the people who need to be there.

If on the other hand you're trying to stay updated with team members who aren't building projects that can conform to a format like that, you may need to adapt a few things. It won't necessarily make sense for there to be a weekly meeting, but there's likely progress that's being made over time, and there needs to be accountability for the progress being made on whatever goals there are. Even if it isn't a "project" per se, there could still likely be a Slack channel, a daily/weekly asynchronous check-in, or others, so that everyone knows at least at a high level what's going on.

It should also be noted that you don't *always* have to stay *fully* up to date on what everyone is working on. It's your job as a manager to assist your team and unblock them when they're stuck; it's not your job to micromanage people and make sure that they're doing things exactly the way that you would be doing them. Especially for the engineers on the team who have a lot of experience and are used to the way that projects are run at the company, it's unlikely that they'll need handholding every step of the way and that you'll need to know exactly what they're working on every single day. This is different if the team skews more junior and people are still getting a feel for how things work, where you'll likely need to be a lot more involved in the projects (or delegate the task of staying up to date with those projects to another engineer on the team who is looking for leadership opportunities).

One of the best things that you can do for your team when you're working remotely is to place trust in them that they will accomplish their goals and complete the projects that they were assigned. It can feel demoralizing when a manager is constantly checking in to make sure that progress is being made on something, which is another reason why it's good to set up processes for engineers to push status updates rather than be prompted for them at random times by their manager.

Types of Calls

When working remotely, it can feel like there's a limited set of options for communicating with your team: you can have a scheduled meeting where you'll talk with each other over a video call, or you can send each other messages on whatever instant messaging platform you use for work. There are other options though, and they may suit your needs better than a plain old video call would. But before diving in to those, we're going to answer the question of whether the video calls that you do host should *actually* involve video or require everyone's cameras to be on.

Video On or Off?

Video on or off, that is the question—and it's a big one! Many people who have turned to remote work have wondered whether it's okay to enforce that their teams always appear on camera while on a call together, or thought about whether it's ethical for their own manager to ask that of them, or considered whether it even matters.

When you're meeting someone in person, there is no option to turn off "video" and prevent everyone that you're talking with from seeing you. So it may feel odd if you're going from an in-person setting where you're used to always working in meetings and being able to see the people that you're talking with to seeing a blank screen or avatar instead and talking at "nothing" on a call without cameras. It can even be disorienting to be speaking and not seeing the usual visual feedback that the person is understanding what is being said and paying attention, or even just being able to tell that the sound is going through to their end and the internet hasn't disconnected. It's definitely a change, and it can take some time to adapt.

The way that some people react to this change is to enforce that everyone always have their video turned on during calls, so that it feels more like talking to a person and not a screen, fostering "deeper connections" between each participant. That's an excuse that I don't believe to be accurate at all: as we talked about in an earlier chapter, people are their most authentic and honest selves when speaking without facing others directly (e.g., when walking side by side or sitting in a car together). If anything, removing people's video from the equation is what could possibly enable those deeper connections.

Connections aside, there are many reasons that someone may not want to turn on their camera during a meeting. For example:

- Their internet speed is slow that day, and they want to make space for the audio (the most important part) to get through.

- Their external camera is acting up and it's a hassle to fix.

- They aren't in the mood to show off their background today, and don't want to deal with virtual backgrounds.

- They're nursing a baby and don't want that on display to their colleagues.

- They just got out of the shower.

- They're in pajamas.

- They're having a bad hair day.

- They're in a public place with a lot of people walking around behind them.

- They feel like slouching.

- They're eating.

- They're pacing around the room which helps them concentrate.

- They're joining the call on a walk outside.

- The call is going to be emotional and they don't want their physical emotions on display.

- Their partner is working from the same room as them and would be visible in the background.

- They just… don't want to.

Whatever their reason is at the moment, if this is a routine meeting between internal parties at a company (and not something like an important external sales meeting), then it's no one's business to know why they aren't enabling their video for the call. They may offer up an explanation, but no one should second-guess it or pry into the reasoning for it. No one is owed the ability to look at their colleagues in their own homes.

On the other hand, why may someone want to talk with their teammates while video is on? While it may be entirely possible to hold most conversations while video is off, there are some that are easier to have while video is on. For example, it might be easier for some (but not all) to talk about more emotionally charged subjects while video is on, especially when someone will be talking for a while while the other is listening, to better see how they're receiving the information instead of waiting for a response at the end (and risking not realizing that the internet actually cut off halfway through their heartfelt outpour). Here are some reasons that some prefer video calls overall:

- The connections they make with colleagues are important to their social lives, and it makes them feel happy to see people's faces which creates stronger bonds.

- The working language is not their native language, and having visual cues and being able to see mouth movements helps them to properly interpret what's being said.

- They have trouble interpreting emotions or recognizing sarcasm from vocal cues, and may look to people's faces and expressions to better understand intention.

- They like seeing how people react to information that they present, especially in long form, getting to see which bits of what they say cause surprise, excitement, or confusion.

- It makes it feel less like they're talking into a void when giving a presentation to a group of people.

- It creates an easier opportunity for small talk ("I love the plants in your background"...) which can make the start of meetings less uncomfortable.

- They're afraid that the meeting will be a waste of time because people will be more likely to distract themselves with other things on their computers since no one can see them glaring off to the side.

There can be just as many reasons for why someone might want to see everyone on video as reasons for why someone might not want to have their camera on.

So whose needs come first? There's always the opportunity for someone to present why they would appreciate it if people were to turn on their cameras if a significant portion of people have disabled them (sometimes, it's off just because of the size of the group), but it shouldn't ever trump the needs of the person with the camera. Everyone has the right to privacy, and unless your job heavily relies on video (which as an engineer it likely doesn't, unless you're managing a team of engineers in Developer Relations who are by definition public-facing), then you should be able to retain the right to keep your camera off for any or all meetings if that's what makes you most comfortable.

There's also a large difference for people in the virtual room when working remotely that isn't present in in-office situations. In Chapter 1, we talked about biases being introduced through remote work because of the look into every employee's personal life that we get through their cameras.

134

This is relevant in hiring, but it doesn't go away after someone has joined a company, even if their equipment has been upgraded and they have a nice setup with fast internet, it's still entirely possible that they don't have the picture-perfect background set up for video calls that others, like executives who may have the time and resources to dedicate to creating such a thing, have. It isn't a great feeling going into a meeting with others who have perfect, clean, and modern backgrounds when you might be sitting at the kitchen counter with the kids' toys scattered around the floor behind you.

Another implication of always having video on is that in larger meetings (think 20+ people), it will actively slow down people's computers because of the amount of processing that is happening and the large amount of incoming data. Reducing the number of people that are visible on the screen can help with this, but then makes it difficult to figure out who is talking at any given point. The best solution for this problem is to reduce the number of people that have video enabled, so that the lag for every individual laptop is lower, and people can engage more with the meeting. And besides, at 20+ people, do you even need to see every person other than those who are in the middle of presenting?

Overall, the topic of video vs. no video is a contentious one with no single blanket solution to cover all cases. As a manager, it's your responsibility to make sure that everyone's work-related needs are being met and that no one feels unnecessarily pressured or otherwise uncomfortable on the topic. It's a good idea to write a team policy outlining what the thoughts on camera vs. no camera are (when it's okay to turn it off, whether it's necessary to have it either way in any situations, etc.). Better yet, share this section of the chapter and all of the explanations of why people may or may not want cameras on, so that everyone on the team can understand the different viewpoints on how cameras might be affecting people who aren't like them. This will help those on your team feel more empowered to turn it off if that's how they would like to work, and it will clear things up for new hires who may otherwise just have to infer those behaviors from others (this goes back to the Chapter 2 on onboarding, and how important it is to have this type of team documentation written).

Tip   An incredibly helpful tip that I learned from my colleague Moni whose first language isn't English is to use the "Closed Captions" feature that many videoconferencing platforms have. This will display the written version of what people are saying on the screen, which helps nonnative speakers to better process what's being said—especially when there's no video to see their mouth movements. This type of aid isn't possible in the same way in a nonremote setting, and is completely invisible: I didn't know she was using it in that way after *hundreds* of meetings together.

The Benefits of Voice-Only

Voice-only calls are actually an entirely different topic than video calls with no video. They put you into an entirely different mindset and form a different style of conversation, and the expectations aren't the same.

Why are they different? It has a lot to do with the settings in which they're used. Video calls are typically *scheduled meetings* that have a prewritten agenda with specific talking points and goals to be achieved. Multiple people block this time off on their calendar and mentally prepare for that time to get together, and be led by the meeting organizer to work toward those goals. Voice-only calls on the other hand are typically spur-of-the-moment and can be joined or left by any group of people at any moment. There's not a lot of planning, there are no talking points, but there's likely a single goal that everyone is working toward in deep problem-solving mode.

In particular when I think of voice-only calls, I think of Discord voice chats or Slack huddles. These are both systems where there's a constant call taking place (metaphorically, not technologically) that you can just drop into and leave whenever you want. No one has to schedule anything, and no links to calls need to be shared. It's always there and available to join, just like how a regular text conversation is always there to write in at any moment. Just because you join the call doesn't mean you'll end up talking to anyone, and you could end up talking into the void the whole time, but it's there!

This might seem like a small thing that doesn't really make a difference up front, and I thought similarly at first too. But removing the need to schedule something and send out links to people just to get a conversation going makes all the difference in the world, especially when there's also no need to mentally prepare yourself to go on video in front of people unexpectedly (if you're currently slouching, you can stay that way without feeling bad about the image you're giving off—I do my best code debugging while slouching heavily). Instead, it becomes extremely easy to send over a quick message to a person or group and say "Hey, can we huddle to work through this?". This ease of communication could mean saving 15 minutes of writing out long-drawn messages that may get misinterpreted, and replacing it with a quick 2-minute voice chat.

In particular, I like to use huddles for pair programming. Often when an engineer on my team gets stuck on a problem, they'll send me or the team a message asking for five minutes of our time to walk through an issue they're solving. They'll share their screens so we're all looking at the same thing, and because there's no video it's easy to focus our mental energy entirely on the code at hand. And since no one had to be explicitly invited, it's easy for other team members to see that we're talking, and jump in on the call to see what's going on. It's like noticing a crowd around someone's desk and joining in. Sometimes, just the mere act of speaking out loud about the problem in a huddle solves it (yay for rubber duck debugging!).

137

I also use this communication method for nonprogramming-related tasks, like when I'm working collaboratively on a slide deck and we're going over the final touches before presenting it (and want all of our attention to be focused on the task at hand), or during incidents. When you're on video, your attention is at least partially focused on how you look, and having that distraction (no matter how unintentional it is) is not a good thing during high-stress moments where full focus is required. Speaking to each other over voice-only calls during incidents is a particularly good example of this, and a great use case. You would just need to make sure that this is happening in a private channel where only the people who need to be involved have access to it; otherwise, you end up in a situation where there are a lot of onlookers that join, which can cause more stress and distract the people working through the incident from actually resolving it (too many cooks in the kitchen!)—something that wouldn't have been an issue with a video call where the necessary people are explicitly invited.

How to Get Started with Voice Chat

One of the tricky things about deploying a voice-only service across a team is that not necessarily everyone will be used to that sort of platform and the etiquette that comes with it (there is etiquette in the same way that video calls have it—like how if you have a lot of background noise, you should go on mute while you aren't talking as to not distract everyone else on the call). This type of calling technology has been around for a while (and while it's similar to phone calls, those are still far more similar to scheduled video calls), but it's been most popular in the gaming world where people would get together and chat voice-only while playing games—where all of their focus is on the game at hand, and it doesn't matter whether they can see each other over video. Because of that, there may be some hesitance or resistance to starting to use voice-only calls as a means to collaborate because it's an unknown. I was one of those people, who resisted adopting it at first because I was so used to connecting over video and didn't understand all the benefits it would bring to the team.

Formalizing the etiquette that you expect of people on the team around voice-only calls, and writing it down as a form of team documentation, will help to make sure that everyone (whether they have experience with platforms like Discord or not) is on the same page about how they're to be used. It should answer questions such as

- Do you need to announce when you're joining or leaving a voice chat?

- Is it okay to just hop into an ongoing chat you see that you have nothing to do with?

- What do you do if you're about to step away from your computer for a few minutes—do you need to announce that you're leaving and will be back?

- What types of conversations are best suited for voice chats as opposed to video calls?

It's the little things, but being explicit about how it works will help people new to it feel more at ease knowing what's expected of them, and it will have a higher likelihood of being adopted.

Embracing Async

Asynchronous communication is when people communicate without an expectation that replies will happen immediately, and instead the information will be parsed and responded to on the receiver's own time when it's convenient for them. For example, exchanging emails is a form of asynchronous communication, but talking on the phone is synchronous communication—since you would in fact expect the other person to engage in the conversation while you're both there.

Async communication isn't anything *new*, but it's something that has been made increasingly popular by remote work because it enables people to embrace the many benefits that remote work has over office life. By defaulting to async, people are more free to schedule their workdays around their life activities and personal preferences: if you know that you can reply to incoming messages at any point during the day, it's easier to make time to go out on a walk in the middle of the afternoon, or grab lunch with a friend. It even makes it easier to travel and work out of a different time zone than usual, because you can reply to everything at shifted hours.

This type of communication can take many forms. While the general idea is that two people don't have to talk in "real time," async communication can mean

- Writing emails.

- Writing comments on documents.

- Sending out meeting agendas.

- Sending voice notes.

- Sending short video messages (e.g., using Loom).

- And even sending messages over platforms like Slack, but it's more difficult to interpret those as async because of the instant message nature of it, especially if they're sent directly to a person and not posted in a broader channel.

While many may claim that they benefit from asynchronous communication, it's often not the case. To some, async means that you're sending each other instant messages instead of talking to each other in "real time" in a scheduled meeting. Those messages, while they may not be urgent or require an answer immediately, do tend to cause anxiety. When you get a notification that you've been sent a message and the barrier to sending them is so low (just type and hit Enter), it's hard to not click in and read them right away, even if they're pulling our focus away from the task at hand. It's gotten so bad that many of us, myself included, will install these same instant messaging platforms on our personal phones so that we can always stay up to date with these messages when we're on the go—going so far as to even check our work messages and emails right before going to bed. This isn't healthy behavior, and it isn't true asynchronous communication either.

The best version of asynchronous communication is when you can send someone a message, and they reply whenever it's convenient for them (within a reasonable timeframe, typically 24 hours to account for time zone differences). Not immediately, and not after their normal work hours. Just whenever they get the chance to do it during the day. To properly achieve this state, it requires full buy-in from everyone on the team. If there's just one person who takes a few hours to answer non-urgent messages and yet everyone else replies instantly, it's going to make that person appear as less dedicated compared to the others even if that isn't the case. Everyone needs to balance their reply times to level the playing field. And by doing this, you'll be allowing everyone more focus time to get their work done. To help with this, normalize muting messaging notifications or emails for blocks of hours at a time, so that you can fully concentrate without always seeing incoming blobs out of the corner of your eye that pull you out of that focus state that's so very much needed to write great code.

When approaching a situation that will require communicating with people, defaulting to an asynchronous-first method is a great idea because it can

- Remove the need to spend time scheduling and attending a meeting.

- Allow people to think through things before replying, leading to better thought-out outcomes.

- Allow people to stay in their focus mode and work uninterrupted, while replying to any incoming messages at a later designated point.

- Improve people's communication skills. Since you don't know when someone might reply, you want to reduce any confusion and the number of back-and-forth messages that might be required to fully discuss something. This means getting the point across clearly and concisely on the first go, which can take practice to build that skill.

Asynchronous communication isn't an all-or-nothing method either: it can be mixed in with synchronous communication too. The recurring check-in workflow mentioned earlier for project updates was a form of fully asynchronous communication, but the example retrospective meeting format covered in Chapter 3 is an example of a combination of the two (the preparation that happens beforehand being the async portion and the actual meeting itself being sync).

While much of the normal work conversations being held can be done as an async-first communication, it's important to note that not *every* conversation should be done in this way. Meetings such as one-on-ones should always be done over a call because their main purpose is to connect and not just deliver information. Some emotionally charged updates such as promotion decisions or difficult feedback should also be done synchronously so that there can be an immediate conversation without either party needing to wait for answers to questions. And some discussions, while technically possible to be held asynchronously, are so complex and require so many fine details that they're best done over a call to reduce confusion and the amount of time spent overall.

Defaulting to async as much as possible means making the most out of remote work for every member of your team, reducing time spent in meetings, and increasing the amount of focus time available. The culture and expectations around it need to be explicitly communicated to the team and exhibited by you too, so that it's clear that it truly is okay to reply to non-urgent messages after a few hours. But the ramp-up time to get the team into that mindset will be worth it!

Takeaways from This Chapter

- A reliance on "water cooler" conversations is a sign of a company that doesn't have proper systems in place for communication and collaboration between teams. Remote teams aren't at a disadvantage from not having this, as long as care is put into thinking through how communication does happen.

- When working with your team, focus on staying updated on the goings-on by using a "push" method and not a "pull" method: make it easy and incentivize them to send you information independently, rather than you constantly asking them for updates and pulling them out of their focused state.

- Set up multiple communication channels for project-based work to accommodate the many types of needs that a team will have over the lifecycle of working together. For example, messaging channels for non-urgent questions and updates, automated bot messages for push-based daily updates, and meetings with proper agendas for in-depth weekly demos and longer form discussion with everyone present.

- If you have a strong team of engineers who are used to the way of working in the company and have familiarity with the tasks they've been assigned, you don't need to know 100% of everything they're doing and the complete status in most circumstances. You've hired highly intelligent engineers to work, so give them the space that they need to complete that work, and you'll end up building more trust in each other.

- There are many reasons why someone might want to keep their camera off during a meeting, and also many reasons why someone might want others to keep theirs on. Have a conversation with the team about what your expectations are around this and write it down, but know that ultimately it is up to each individual to determine whether or not they will be turning on their camera because no one has the obligation to be able to look into the personal homes and see someone when they don't want to be seen.

- Voice-only calls are a great way to get work done without the overhead of creating and sharing links to join video calls, or worrying about how you look on camera. They allow you to intensely focus on the task at hand, and are in particular terrific for pair programming and incident resolution.

- Write up a document for your team on voice call etiquette since it's likely a new technology for many people. It will clear up its intended use, and will make people feel more at ease, increasing the likelihood that the technology will be adopted.

- Async communication does not mean just using Slack instead of a video call. It requires a commitment from everyone on the team to only reply to messages when it's convenient for them and not pulling their focus away from their work. This means not receiving replies instantly, but also not being constantly distracted by the incoming notifications. It requires a cultural shift

and everyone needs to be on the same page so that
no one person is the odd one out and appears to be
slacking off while everyone else is replying to messages
instantly. This is also something that could be written
in team documentation to set the standards.

CHAPTER 7

Feedback and Promotions

Giving your team members feedback on a regular basis is a major part of your job as a manager. When done right, feedback is a gift that can help your direct reports grow in their careers and work toward their long-term goals. It's equally important to give both praise for work that has been done well and constructive feedback to help guide people toward continuous improvement. And while feedback is so critical to both teams and individuals, it can be very difficult to *give* meaningful feedback, and can also be extremely difficult to *receive* in a way that encourages people to give even more in the future.

Feedback can be given at any point in time (e.g., timely feedback after something occurs), but also on a regular cycle typically enforced by the company such as a year-end review cycle, a quarterly performance review, or even a 360-degree feedback cycle. Some companies even skip the yearly review in favor of more frequent monthly check-ins with smaller doses of feedback. There's no one way to do it that works for all companies or teams, but it's a delicate matter overall and dreaded by many because of how easy it is to give poor and non-actionable feedback, and how difficult it is to receive feedback well. Often, the official feedback cycles are tied in with the promotion and salary adjustment cycles, because the "rating" received from your manager and peers reflects your perceived standing in the organization.

© Alexandra Sunderland 2022
A. Sunderland, *Remote Engineering Management*,
https://doi.org/10.1007/978-1-4842-8584-8_7

In this chapter, we'll cover how to approach giving feedback in a remote organization, how to create a culture of feedback on your team, and how to make sure that promotions are approached in a fair manner and the remote-based biases to look out for when making those career-changing decisions. We'll also look at how a lot of the emotional and communication difficulties around feedback can be exacerbated when you don't share a physical office with your team, but how some aspects of remote work can also make the whole exchange easier for everyone involved.

How to Give Great Feedback

There are a few aspects of giving feedback that make it especially useful: it has to be timely, and it has to be specific—whether it's for praise or for constructive feedback.

Timely feedback is when you're giving feedback before too much time has passed after the event you're giving feedback on, and at the right time. If someone is demoing their code and they seem very unprepared, you wouldn't stop them mid-presentation to let them know—you'd wait until after when you were both alone to give them a heads-up about the issue and its impact. But if someone presented some sort of incredible new feature, you would praise them in front of everyone in that meeting instead of waiting to do it privately.

Praise in public, criticize in private.

In both cases, the timing of the feedback's delivery was different, but the timeliness was correct given the different situations. Being as specific as possible helps both types of feedback land properly too: knowing that "you did a great job with the presentation" is not particularly helpful when there are so many aspects to presenting, just as "you should work on your presentation skills" isn't particularly helpful either. The specific aspects that went well or didn't go so well should be called out ("you paced yourself and presented your arguments clearly," or "you were looking down at your feet and didn't engage with the audience") so that people know what they need to change next time or what in particular they should continue to do to be successful.

When working remotely, it might seem a little tricky to stay timely in all situations—especially if you're working in a different time zone as the person who will be receiving the feedback, and the feedback is about some sort of asynchronous interaction (e.g., the tone of an email or the level of detail in a documentation page). It's not possible to just pull someone aside in the hall after they've given a presentation when you're remote.

Choosing the Appropriate Delivery Method

To start off, something that you should know about each of your direct reports is how they prefer to receive feedback. This is something that I recommend finding out about them in your very first one-on-one together.

There are a few different ways of receiving feedback: through written messages, voice-only calls, video calls, recorded video messages, etc. The two main factors though are in figuring out whether they prefer to receive feedback in written or auditory format, and whether they prefer for it to be coming from you in real time or sent to be listened to asynchronously on their own time, when they're ready. It can be tough to receive constructive feedback, and it can elicit strong emotional responses—because even though it comes with the best of intentions, there's no getting away from the fact that they're hearing about something they did imperfectly. Receiving it as a recorded message can make it easier to process the emotions around it while alone, and think through it fully before asking questions or responding so that you aren't caught up in the moment. It also gives them the chance to choose when they're ready to listen to it: people aren't always in the right mindset to hear constructive feedback, and will absorb the information better at a later time. Knowing people's preferences for this allows the delivered feedback to be received in the most effective way for them possible.

Going off of the team's preferences doesn't have to be applied for *everything* though, just the day-to-day non-urgent feedback. If someone is consistently having performance issues or there's a serious problem at hand and you need to have a conversation and ensure that they're properly understanding the importance of the feedback, it's fine to override any known preferences and deliver it in real time. A kind thing to do when giving feedback to someone on work product is to ask them first, "are you open to receiving feedback on this," because they might not be in the right mindset to receive it, and it gives them the space to ask for it to be given later.

On the timing of the delivery of feedback in remote work, there are a few options:

- If the feedback is very pertinent to a situation at hand (someone did a great job in something that you both experienced at the same time, like in a meeting), then the feedback should be given as soon as possible. Both of you will still have all the relevant details of the situation top of mind, so it will land the most effectively. If the feedback is along the lines of "you lost the crowd in this section of the presentation, aim to make it more engaging," then it'll be a lot harder for them to mentally go back to that moment in a week and understand where the feedback might be coming from and what they could do differently next time.

- For all other feedback (from asynchronous interactions, or non-urgent general feedback that isn't pertinent to any one given situation), the best option is to talk about it in your next one-on-one, which hopefully is within the next week as we talked about in the chapter about them. If they prefer to receive feedback asynchronously or it's the type of thing that should be shared earlier, you can send them a message or recorded video, or ask them if they have a minute to receive some feedback over a call.

Tip   One of the scariest messages someone can get from their manager is "Can we talk?". If you have feedback that needs to be delivered to someone as soon as possible and don't want to give it in writing, ask instead "Do you have a few minutes to talk? I have some feedback about X that I'd like to share."

Structuring Feedback to Be Effective

When providing feedback, especially constructive feedback that has the potential to be emotional, thought should be put into the structure of what will be said, so that enough information is provided up front to try to take it from an emotionally charged feedback discussion to a rational and factual one that gets the message across. Sometimes, all you want to say is something along the lines of "Stop interrupting me when I talk, it drives me nuts," but formulating it like that is only going to get a reaction out of the person, who will not respond in a particularly useful or receptive way—because their sense of belonging is being threatened with the combative way that it's made to sound like they're not a good person overall. Instead, taking the time to structure feedback will help the recipient process the information, and it will demonstrate that the intent is to help them improve, and not to criticize.

A popular structure for feedback is the *Situation-Behavior-Impact* model (or SBI for short). This framework can be used for both positive and constructive feedback, and involves the following three components:

- **Situation:** Where and when the behavior in question took place. For example, in a given meeting, over a particular email chain, on a call, ...

- **Behavior:** An objective description of what took place, and what the feedback is about.

- **Impact:** The impact the behavior had, in a noncombative way. Avoid describing what the person may have done wrong, and focus on the impact that it had on the affected people. For example, "the team had a hard time following the presentation" comes across more kindly than "your presentation was hard to follow."

Using the SBI model, the feedback from earlier ("Stop interrupting me when I talk, it drives me nuts") could be delivered more effectively like this: "In the team meeting earlier today *(situation)*, you often started talking over me when I wasn't finished *(behavior)*. I was hurt by this, and it made me feel like my opinions aren't valued *(impact)*. I would appreciate it if you waited for me to finish speaking before starting to talk."

The same formula applies for positive feedback too. Positive feedback is great for reinforcing behaviors and showing people that they should continue to do something, but they need to be aware of specifically which aspects of the thing they did that should be replicated. While telling someone they did a "great job" is positive feedback and will make them feel good, it isn't all that useful because they won't know which aspect in particular made it good that they should continue to replicate in the future.

Bonusly recommends including an extra step in this framework when delivering constructive feedback: *exploration*.[1] They point out that because constructive (or negative) feedback is meant to help people grow instead of knocking them down, it's helpful to explore with the recipient what caused the situation to occur in the first place, and how to make things better together. This also brings the benefit of enabling the person to be less defensive about the feedback they're receiving, because they'll be able to see that you really do have their best interest at heart.

After Delivering Feedback

The process of giving someone constructive feedback isn't over when the message has been delivered! There are a few steps that can be taken to make sure that the feedback gets implemented:

- **Ask them what they think:** They may have an entirely different view on what's going on, and might disagree with the feedback but not feel empowered to say so unless asked. Approaching the feedback process with empathy for the recipient and trying to get their perspective on it allows for it to be more fair. At times, I've given feedback to people about things I was so sure about, only for them to provide context I wasn't aware of and entirely change the way I thought about the situation. This is especially relevant in remote work where a lot of context is hidden behind the scenes.

- **Deliver it in multiple methods:** Everyone processes information differently, including feedback. After the initial feedback has been given according to the recipient's preferred method, its fair game to deliver it

---

[1] https://blog.bonus.ly/feedback-examples

in other mediums. Whenever I deliver feedback over calls with members of my team, I then write it down in our shared one-on-one note too so that they can revisit it. I process information visually, and information doesn't quite land right when I only hear it, so having feedback available both in written and verbal format ensures that others like me are able to process feedback equally with their peers.

- **Follow up:** When you've delivered critical feedback, updating that person on their future behaviors is as important as that initial conversation. If someone has acted on the feedback and their behaviors now match what is expected, let them know that you've noticed and that you appreciate the change! If the same pattern as before is continuing though, the feedback may not have gotten through to them, and it might be time to revisit the conversation.

Creating a Culture of Feedback

Feedback doesn't only need to be given by you to your direct reports, it should regularly be exchanged in both directions and between you and your peers too. And just as important as giving thoughtfully structured feedback is being able to receive it well without becoming defensive.

How to Receive Feedback

Being able to listen to and act on feedback as a manager is one of the most important aspects in creating a strong culture of feedback on your team. People will look to how you react and how you solicit feedback to inform what's expected of them in those same situations. If you're becoming defensive by deflecting feedback, explaining it away, or reacting with anger or confusion, people will not enjoy giving you feedback, and it will teach them not to give any—and then even when you're explicitly asking for some, they won't be honest with you out of fear of the resulting reaction. Not receiving feedback well as a manager is doing a disservice to both yourself and the entire team, because your ability to absorb feedback is a major factor in your growth as a manager.

When someone is providing you with feedback, whether solicited or not, the best way to respond is to listen attentively to their thoughts. Whether or not it's true and whether you agree with it is irrelevant: it might have taken them a lot of courage to bring it up, especially given that they're giving critical feedback to the person that has a lot of influence over their career and compensation. They should be rewarded for that courage with a positive reception, so that they continue to provide their thoughts in the future—otherwise, you'll end up with a team that never tells you when you're doing something wrong, and that'll stunt your own career growth in addition to creating a stagnant team environment.

When you're being given feedback, listen to what's being said attentively. Don't interrupt, and don't deny what's being said. Even if what they're saying isn't accurate, it appears to be true from their point of view, and so it *is* the truth for them, and that's worth acknowledging. If they're saying something along the lines of "You're always in meetings so you never have time to help us, and that bothers me because it takes longer to accomplish certain tasks," but you know that you only spend five hours per week in meetings, their feedback isn't invalid. What they're actually saying is that you aren't making it clear enough that you have time available to help people, and that you should do more to advertise that fact. The wrong reaction would be to argue on the technicality of the true amount time spent in meetings. When they're done providing the feedback, thank them! Let them know that what they've said is valuable, and that you hope that they continue to bring you those insights in the future. By showing that you truly do appreciate what they've said, they'll leave the conversation feeling good about it instead of nervous that they just criticized "the boss," and will be on the lookout for more opportunities for that in the future. You can also ask some follow-up clarifying questions coming from a perspective of curiosity, like the extra "exploration" step in the SBI process described earlier.

Being Transparent

One of my favorite ways to foster a strong culture of feedback on the team is by soliciting and responding to feedback in the open. This doesn't always mean just asking people out loud in a team meeting if they have any thoughts for me (although sometimes it does), you still have to take a meticulous approach to how you ask for feedback to make it useful and easy to give.

One of the best ways of doing this without needing to label it as feedback per se is through implementing recurring retrospectives, which we covered in depth in Chapter 3. Retrospectives are meetings that are entirely based on collecting and talking through feedback about things in general, and they're an extremely powerful tool. After I run a retrospective, I always follow it up with a feedback survey sent out to everyone that attended. It includes easy-to-answer questions like "Yes or No, did you find that meeting useful?" and "Do you think the amount of time we spent on the retro was too much, too little, or just right?", followed by some open-ended yet pointed questions. You'll receive little (if any) feedback if you point-blank ask "Do you have any feedback or comments?", but will get much more useful and detailed answers if you qualify the question with more specificity—like "What do you think about how we did X?"—because it prompts people to think about something in particular.

After everyone has sent in their feedback, I take the data and aggregate it all into graphs. Those graphs represent the overall answers to each question, with anonymized data. I put those graphs into the next team meeting's agenda, along with the key points from the free-form text questions that have been rewritten by me so that no one can tell who wrote each answer based on the style of writing. We then go over those results together, and I talk about the changes that will be implemented in the next retro to address the items. It's like a retro to the retro! This feedback has been instrumental in adapting that particular meeting process over the years. Each time we run the survey, we reuse the same multiple-choice questions so that we can track trends over time and see if we're on the right path toward keeping it a valuable meeting. But by presenting this feedback to everyone and being totally transparent about what everyone had to say, the culture around feedback is really being built up. Sometimes, what's written is negative, and it would be so easy for me to just keep it to myself and hide away the comments for how I can be better at running it. But instead I show in front of everyone that I truly appreciate what they had to say, show how I'm planning on changing, and then they can see me follow through on that in the next retro. It's a great cycle of requesting for feedback, listening to it, and really responding to it by implementing changes.

That kind of behavior is what encourages people to continuously give feedback, because they know that it won't be passed aside or held against them. It's what's encourages people on the team to give feedback to each other and respond in similar ways. And when we're all giving each other feedback on our work, we're all making each other better, we all grow, and we're better off as a team.

I often run similar surveys for the other recurring meetings that I host so that I can make sure we're always making the best use of our time together. And often, the responses will be entirely different than what I was expecting they'd be. There's a twice-weekly team meeting that I thought for sure everyone would want to get rid of so they could get a half hour of their morning back, but every single person said it was one of their favorite meetings, and they absolutely do not want to get rid of it. It's so great to be able to get honest feedback so that we aren't making uninformed decisions that aren't in the best interest of our team.

To get started in creating this culture on your team, start by finding something that you can ask for feedback about—you likely won't get many helpful answers if you just ask for feedback in general. Start by asking about specific processes, meetings, or even parts of the code. Once you've built up that trust that you will react in a positive manner, you can start venturing into asking for feedback on how you conduct certain aspects of your work, and start growing yourself.

Ensuring That Promotions Are Fair

It's likely that even if you aren't exchanging feedback with your team on a weekly basis, you at least have a once-per-year feedback process where you get to collect feedback on each direct report from their peers, have them fill out a self-evaluation form, and then provide them with the summarized feedback on top of your own as a wrap-up to the year. This conversation might even include goal setting for the next year, and it very likely includes discussions around promotions—or at the very least, the conversations that happen during it will feed into the promotion and compensation decisions. That's part of why having these conversations and doing them right is so important; they highly impact people's careers and lives.

At the very least, dedicate two to three hours *per direct report* to read through their feedback and write your own. It will feel like an incredibly large amount of work (especially if you have a large team), but so much of your role as a manager is to help people grow in their career, and it's a small time investment to get to that goal when scaling back and looking at it from the perspective of time invested doing this for the entire year.

Learning About the Hidden Work

Something that is particularly difficult no matter what style of office environment you have (remote or not) is getting a proper view into how someone truly works and the impact they have on the company, in a nonbiased way. It's easy to keep tabs on the people that you may have a stronger relationship with, or are building the types of things that you like to build, or are more vocal about their successes (or have people who are very vocal on their behalf). It's much harder to properly stay up to date with all the amazing work that those who are less vocal about their accomplishments are doing. Does talking about your own success less mean that you're less successful in the workplace and having less impact on the company than others? It can certainly appear that way. People get promoted based on job performance, and *perception*. You want to promote the people who are perceived well on the team, because those who are trying to reach that same level will try to emulate their characteristics in hopes of promotion too. But just because someone is more reserved does not mean that they aren't accomplishing just as much as those who are shouting it from the virtual rooftop.

Underrepresented groups in engineering are more likely to be reserved about their successes, play things down out of "humbleness," or give credit to others for their own work. I'm still trying to unlearn all of those behaviors myself. The discussion around this could be (and likely is) an entire book; there are so many factors and things that come into play when discussing certain people's experience in the workplace that we don't have space to discuss here. But we can talk about strategies for making sure that promotions and feedback are as fair to everyone as possible, regardless of how loud each individual is about their own accomplishments.

My first tip is something that you can do yourself, but also actually encourage your team members to take on themselves. It's extremely important for people to be in charge of their own growth and stand up for themselves, especially as they become more senior in their careers. This means being able to recognize what they need and want to grow new skills in, where they need improvement, and what they're excellent at which (the skills of which they should be attempting to use as much as possible). Every January, I create a "You Got This" document for the year where I'll jot down notes throughout the year with all of the highlights and things that I'm proud of, and quotes from feedback or praise I've received that make me happy. I include a few headers that are generally relevant to the types of things that I like to work on so that it looks a little organized—things like *"Things I did that I'm proud of," "Times you acted like a leader,"* and *"Obstacles you overcame and things that were scary."* In that last one, I like to include non-work things too: one year I included that I rode a scary rollercoaster that I had avoided for years, another year I talked about how I skied down my first black diamond run when I thought it would be too steep for me, because they were both scary challenges that opened me up to new experiences and personal growth. This year, I'm including writing this book! I'll add things to the list as soon as they happen, because I know that realistically I'll forget about them really quickly, and will have an incredibly hard time remembering all the great things I did in January when I'm writing my self-review in December—and if even *I* don't remember what I did, how can I expect *my manager* to?

That very question is what led me to try an experiment with the team of interns that we had hired one summer. I decided that I would create my own "You Got This" note for each of them, aptly named "Summeries" (a summary of their summer at the company). Starting from day one, I would make note of any feature they built, any great demo they did at a team meeting, and any time that they went above and beyond. It was keeping tabs on how they were progressing, which was terrific for me since I didn't feel that I had to keep all of those items in my working memory. During our final one-on-ones in the last week of their internships, I sent them these Summeries to keep as memories and to act as a list of their own accomplishments to help them understand just how much impact they had had at the company. The best part? They had completely forgotten about all the things they had done too—and they were only there for four months.

If we're able to so easily forget our own accomplishments, you can imagine that managers (who will forget their own) won't necessarily have the best idea of exactly what each of their multiple direct reports did throughout the year. There will be the highlight reel of major accomplishments that they can hopefully dig up in their memory for each person, but it can be tricky to remember everything that you need in order to give proper feedback and prepare to put people up for promotions. Additionally, a lot of the work that people do is not visible to their manager: if you're helping people solve problems and creating documentation or doing anything that doesn't directly involve your manager, the only way that they'll find out what you're doing and how much impact it has is if you or someone impacted by it tells them, because it's so awkward to go yourself to your manager and say "hey, I'm doing this awesome thing, look"—especially when you've been conditioned to not speak of yourself in that way.

This is exacerbated in a remote environment, where people are less likely to talk about all the smaller things that they're doing in open channels that you'll read through. I've found out many, many times from people on my team that others on the team are doing an incredible amount of extra work that's extremely valuable to the team, but they just weren't bringing it up—nor was I asking them about it, because there was no negative impact to their main work and so there was no reason for me to think that they were taking on large amounts of extra work. That was my first mistake: I now often ask people in our one-on-ones what they've worked on or contributed in the last few weeks that I might not know about, so that they have the space to talk about those extra activities without needing the courage to bring it up themselves and feel like they're bragging.

I now also encourage my team members to start their own "You Got This" note every year so that they can also keep track of their own accomplishments. It's so useful for the end-of-year feedback cycle when they're writing their self-review, but it's also a terrific note to have when you're feeling down. If you're someone that's prone to imposter syndrome (feeling as though you don't belong and someone will "find out" that you're a fraud), having that kind of material to read through can be strongly uplifting because it provides concrete proof that you do know what you're doing, and you do belong.

Promotion Negotiation

Promotion time becomes easier when all my direct reports have those kinds of notes available (and I have my own notes of the truly exceptional things they've done throughout the year) because they're able to articulate for themselves what they want, why they want it, and *why they deserve it* using the information they've been keeping track of all year. Ultimately, as a manager it's your job to do this promotion negotiation on behalf of them with whoever the final decision maker is, but I believe that it's also your job to grow them and help them be successful in any future jobs they may have too.

Not every manager will be the type to stick up for their team unfortunately (and by virtue of you reading this book, we can assume you're the type that *would* stick up for them), and so being able to advocate on behalf of yourself is a very useful skill to have in the workplace. Even if I'll be the one doing the negotiating for them, whether it comes to title or salary, I always have my direct reports go over their own pitch with me to build up that muscle—and there's another benefit for them too: they know more about themselves and their work than I do; it's likely that you'll learn something else that you can then use on their behalf. Being up front about why you're doing this is key, and it helps to build trust with them because they'll know that you're looking out for them not just in their current role but also for whenever they eventually leave and need to negotiate their new salaries elsewhere.

When working remotely, all of this is especially important. When people do that extra work like helping out their teammates or debugging tough issues, you won't necessarily see it happening. It might be over video calls you aren't invited to, in Slack channels you didn't know exist. It's all happening, but there's no way for you to be aware of it without someone telling you. If you were in an office, it'd be easier to pick up on it because you might be able to overhear people talking, or see someone swivel their chair over to their teammate and spend time at their desk going over code together. When remotely, it's just that much more important to make space for people to tell you about all the great things they're doing and impact that they're having on the team, and making sure that you're not being influenced by the recency bias when looking back at what they've done throughout the year.

With those tips, you'll be able to have a more clear view of what people are accomplishing and what their work product is. With that information, you can make better decisions around compensation and promotions, because you aren't just relying on the loudest people in the room to understand the full picture of what's going on in the remote workplace.

Announcing Promotions

And lastly, when someone is promoted or receives a title change on the team, make sure to announce it at both the next team meeting and over whatever instant messaging tool you use! The team meeting makes it feel official, and the people can see others excited and clapping for them which gives a strong positive emotional response, while the written message is likely to bring on many happy emoji reactions, and gives them something to screenshot and add to that "You Got This" note to look back on later when they're feeling down.

Takeaways from This Chapter

- Giving and asking for feedback is one of the most important things that you can do as a leader, and one of the things that is the most likely to make your team better overall and everyone as individuals.

- Giving feedback can often be tied to official feedback or performance review cycles, but it should be given often outside of those structures as well so that everyone is constantly getting better and seeing their work be appreciated.

- When giving feedback, whether critical or praise, it's important to be specific and timely. Vague statements like "You were great" may feel good, but aren't helpful to the person receiving the feedback in understanding how they could get better or what they should continue doing.

- In your first one-on-ones, ask your direct reports how they like to receive feedback (written, verbal, real time, async, …) so that it lands properly with them and reduces the emotional response to it.

- The best way to format feedback for it to land properly is "Situation"/"Behavior"/"Impact." This applies both to constructive and positive feedback. It makes sure that people understand exactly what aspect of their behavior they should continue doing or change and why it's important.

- To create a strong culture around feedback on your team, ask for feedback and share aggregated and anonymized results in the open to demonstrate that you truly appreciate it and are doing something about what's mentioned. Start by requesting feedback about specific processes or meetings, and then you can venture into asking about specific attributes of yourself once you've gained trust that you won't react negatively.

- Create a "You Got This" note every year and encourage your team members to as well. In this note, add all of your accomplishments, quotes from teammates, obstacles you overcame, and anything else you want. It's a great resource for writing performance reviews because it avoids the recency bias, and helps to lift you up on days that you're feeling down.

- Ask "what have you done this week that I might not know about" in your one-on-ones so that your team members (especially those who might not be very self-promotional) have a space to talk about the impact they're having on the team that you may not be noticing because of the team being remote. This helps to create a more equitable way of viewing everyone's accomplishments, because not everyone will be equally vocal about them otherwise.

- Even if you'll be the person negotiating someone's compensation adjustment or promotion, have that person practice doing that for themselves with you. It will build up a strong negotiation muscle that they will need to use in future workplaces where their manager doesn't stick up for people as much, and it gives you more insight into their work that you can then also use in your negotiations for them. Be up front about how this is for their own development, and it'll help build trust with them.

CHAPTER 8

Burnout

When working in an office with someone in person, over time you start
to understand their typical mood patterns and learn to pick up on certain
behavioral cues that convey their current mental and emotional state. For
example, you might recognize when they're stressed out or tired because
of the subtleties of their interactions with others or the amount of coffee
they're drinking; or you might notice when something must be going really
well in their lives too. When working remotely, those cues don't exist in
the same way and are much more subtle: you typically aren't seeing how
someone carries themselves throughout the day, and interactions are
limited to text-based messages or meetings. This can be a very good thing,
especially for those who don't necessarily want to be sharing how they're
feeling with those around them at work or bring attention to themselves if
something is wrong. But it can also have its downsides, because when we
aren't able to pick up on the fact that something is going wrong, we can't
help out.

As humans, we're naturally very social creatures and we stick together.
When one of us is feeling down, we come together to help them out. At an
office, this might look like someone inviting you to the coffee shop for tea,
or delivering a fresh pastry to your desk—or even just dropping by to say
hi and see how you're doing. Remotely, it's harder: unless you're getting
creative, your options are mostly limited to dropping into a chat or call to
talk. I've been lucky enough to have had people send me pastries on both
happy and sad occasions, and I've dropped off or ordered surprises for

© Alexandra Sunderland 2022
A. Sunderland, *Remote Engineering Management*,
https://doi.org/10.1007/978-1-4842-8584-8_8

special moments in the lives of my team members—but it comes at the strange cost of asking for someone's address, which is quite personal. The signals that we look for to understand how our peers are doing change significantly when we're working remotely. This is important to know and understand as a manager, because when your team isn't feeling quite right, they don't work as well together, and little issues can snowball into larger cracks in the team's foundation.

And while it's great to care about the people on your team and how they're doing in their personal lives, I do want to make the following clear:

You are not responsible for your team members' personal lives, you are only responsible for them at work.

If there's only one lesson you take away from this chapter, let that be it.

There is a little bit of overlap, but ultimately you should not be problem-solving their lives and interfering beyond what is acceptable. The line is blurry and will vary from person to person: some might not want you to know about any personal details; others might cry in your one-on-ones when they share the hardships they're going through. It's normal to feel empathy for people—and if you're a manager, you're likely quite empathetic already—but by the nature of your work relationship, *you are not friends or family*. It's perfectly fine to have a friendly relationship, but at the end of the day, it's still professional: you will always be seen as the "boss." It's healthy to keep boundaries, as much as your problem-solving instincts might try to kick in. It took me *years* to learn this, and I'm still not perfect at it. When someone shares something with me, I need to actively fight the urge to start proposing solutions or involving myself too much. But it's better for your own mental health to keep those boundaries: taking on the emotional burden of a whole team's personal problems is a lot to deal with and weighs heavily—it's not fair to you, and it's not fair to the team that then has an emotionally exhausted manager.

It should be noted though that a lack of problem-solving does not mean avoiding providing accommodations. If your team member tells you that they are feeling down and overwhelmed because they are caring for a sick loved one, the proper response is not to nod and carry on. There are many cases where you can discuss what could be done at work to better accommodate their situation and make it easier for them to accomplish their goals while dealing with their personal situation—for example, adjusting work hours, lightening the load, moving them onto a different project, or taking time off.

While hopefully when something is going wrong in someone's personal life they'll be up front that they might need accommodations, they might not be so candid when it's something at work that's going wrong, out of fear of appearing to not be good at their job—something that can contribute to burnout. In this chapter, we'll talk about how to spot the signs of burnout from both your team members and yourself, how to prevent people from getting to that point, and how to provide accommodations and recover.

What Is Burnout?

When someone works far too much, has a lot of stress at work, and in general has a lot being asked of them, they're at risk for burnout. Being burned out is more than just being tired after a long week at work: it's being so physically and mentally exhausted for a long period of time that their personal life suffers too, and a vacation alone won't fix it.

Burnout symptoms and effects can include

- Constant exhaustion and fatigue, even when not working

- Negativity or reluctance toward work and hobbies that were previously enjoyable

- Procrastination, low motivation, and a lack of focus on even simple tasks at work and at home

- Irritability and unwarranted anger

- Social isolation

These aren't nice symptoms to have! It can look like someone is just a poorly performing employee, when usually burnout is the result of someone dedicating far too much time and effort to the company, then suffering the consequences through their own deteriorated health, and having the opposite desired effect in the end. Burnout can take *months* to recover from, and it isn't as simple as taking a week or two of vacation to rest and relax. Once the damage has been done, it can be a long time before someone gets back to their normal state of flow pre-burnout.

Burnout is a state that you want to avoid at all costs, both for yourself and for the people on your team. And while you might be able to recognize the symptoms and warning signs in yourself, there is far less information about how someone else is feeling and whether they're getting close to burnout too when working remotely where interactions are limited. On top of that, people that work from home are prime candidates for developing it: since remote workers are often working from their homes, the boundaries between work and life are blurred, and work can end up spilling over where it shouldn't and not leaving enough time for proper rest.

How to Spot Burnout in Your Team

So how do you spot it then? Especially when you're only interacting with people a few times per week over calls, maybe here and there on Slack and over pull request reviews and ticket comments, and not sitting next to them day to day and seeing the trends over time of how they're appearing to be at work and how they interact with those around them. There are some signs to look out for, but there are no surefire ways. No matter what, it requires having a good understanding of what "normal" is. And if you're a manager with fewer than ten or so people on your team, this is something that should be reasonably achievable. You can't establish a baseline of what someone's "normal" looks like overnight (and especially not in the first few weeks of someone's time on your team because of how they'll be specifically trying to go above and beyond to ramp up quickly, like we went over in Chapter 2), but after a few months, you will come to an understanding of what someone's normal communication and behavioral patterns are. Knowing that, here are some things to look out for.

Look Out for: Communication Patterns

Changes in communication patterns are some of the biggest changes to look out for on a remote team, but can also be some of the trickiest since communication happens in so many different ways, and in so many different formats (as we saw in Chapter 6).

Look out for changes in the frequency of messages sent, the tone of the messages (going from bright and happy to to-the-point or dismissive), lateness to meetings, the amount of talking done in meetings, or the way that information is offered up (do they only answer questions directed at them, or do they give updates like they normally do). There are no particular styles of communication to look out for as a signal for burnout, because one person's burnout signal could be another person's completely normal way of communicating.

Look Out for: Work Patterns

Shifts in work patterns are the next biggest change to look out for. While someone might have a good reason for doing so, if a person who normally wraps up their day at 5pm and spends time with their family is now pushing error-filled commits at 10pm and not properly updating the tickets that they were normally so on top of, that's a bit of an odd change.

It could be a temporary blip because of a huge deadline and a project that was poorly planned that they absolutely do not want to finish late; it could be that they have a newborn and the only time they get to code is at nighttime because they're sleeping during the day. It could be any number of reasons. But if it doesn't make sense, or it persists beyond a "one-off instance" amount of time, then it's time to investigate!

Look Out for: Engagement Patterns

A reduced level of interest in the work that they're taking on is the third signal that you can spot as their manager. If someone is normally very engaged with their project—asking a lot of questions, giving updates, seemingly enthusiastic, and doing research into the problem at hand— then slowly becomes disinterested, and is looking just to accomplish the task at its bare minimum without any of the excitement that they normally would exhibit, that can be a clear sign of burnout—and is encompassed by both the change in communication and work patterns. Interest levels can of course vary from project to project, and we've all had to take on our fair share of boring projects, so this is also very up to judgment on the situation at hand.

How to Talk About It

If you spot any of these signs in someone, don't let it slide and hope that things will get better on their own; it will likely require some action on both your and their part to make things better, so it's best to talk about it sooner rather than later.

The conversation around this is best had in a one-on-one (you wouldn't want to burn them out even more by scheduling yet another meeting on their calendar), and should come from a place of curiosity. It's not possible to know whether they are burned out or if there's something else going on behind the scenes—such as factors external to them at work that are causing them harm, or something going on in their life outside of work. You don't want to approach the conversation accusing them of being burned out and blaming them for poor work performance; that won't help the situation no matter what the reasoning behind their behaviors is. Start by asking how they're doing before mentioning the changes that you've noticed in them (whether it's the change in communication patterns, work patterns, or level of interest) with examples. They might open up and talk about challenges they've been having—which is great, you can work toward rectifying the problem!

The tricky thing is that a lot of these symptoms can also look like underperformance. The main difference is that you're only noticing these symptoms because they're out of the ordinary, and the person was supposedly not like this before, so you know that they are good performers. It might be hard to tell the two apart. But it's good to have the conversation with them to understand whether they're tired, the projects they've been assigned just aren't right for them, or even if they're just getting bored with what they're working on—a sign that they may start to think about leaving the team soon if they haven't already been looking around.

No matter what though, burnout will not go away on its own, and it's necessary to address it when you think you see it for the sake of the team and the mental health of that person.

How to Spot Burnout in YOU

Figuring out whether YOU are burned out is a bit different than it is when you're trying to determine whether someone on your team is burned out—simply because you have access to so much more information about how you're really feeling, and what is causing you to feel that way. The tactics used to identify changes in other people might not even be suitable when looking at oneself, because we're less likely to be able to pick up on changes in our own communication or work patterns, especially if the shift is gradual.

So how do you figure out whether you're on the slippery slope to burnout without waiting for someone to point it out to you? Well there won't likely be one particular morning where you wake up and think to yourself "I'm now burned out!". It's far more likely that it will be a gradual shift in attitudes about everything and energy levels until it eventually becomes such a hindrance to daily life that it can't be ignored anymore. But before getting to that point, be on the lookout for the symptoms mentioned earlier in the chapter. While it's normal to have an off week here and there or be particularly tired out if there's a big deadline coming up, being consistently pessimistic about work, too exhausted to even do hobbies that bring you joy, and trying to avoid work at all costs are all signs that you're on a bad path.

The Importance of Filling Your Own Cup

If you're feeling this way, please seek help! Whether it's friends, family, a trusted colleague, or a professional therapist, the first step to making changes and recovering is talking about it with someone. Burnout can cause lasting damage and take a physical toll, and no amount of advice that I could write in this book is a replacement for going over the particularities of your situation with someone and devising a tailored plan. It's so important to avoid burnout and have the mental energy as a manager because our jobs revolve around helping other people—but we can't do that with an empty cup.

Preventing Burnout

While it's terrific to catch burnout before it takes too strong of a hold on anyone, it's even better to prevent it (and general workplace stress) in the first place.

Following are some tips on how you can set the team up for success and try to help prevent anyone from getting on the path to burnout. These are strategies that you can use yourself, and communicate out to your team as good habits to instill early to keep a healthy harmony of work life at home.

Reduce Notifications

Turn off notifications for all work-related messaging and emails on your personal devices after work hours. Better yet, don't have work-related apps on your personal devices at all! It's so easy to fall into the habit of checking Slack or email right before going to bed, and first thing when you wake up. It makes it difficult to keep boundaries around work time, and makes it so that you never fully disconnect from work to focus on the other aspects of your life. Muting notifications and doing it in such a way that makes it clear that you're on "Snooze" shows to others on the team that you're disconnected, and that it's okay for them to do that too. This small action will help to establish a culture of healthy work/life balance on the team, beyond the immediate benefits to yourself.

Work Life and Personal Life Separation

Schedule time for activities away from screens during your workday. If you were in an office, you wouldn't be working eight hours straight at your desk without any breaks whatsoever. You'd get up a few times to walk to the coffee machine, go to the washroom, maybe even walk down the block to pick up lunch and then sit with your colleagues to have a break from your desk. There's no reason that you can't do the same when working from home! It can be harder to convince yourself that it's okay to get up from your desk (you might miss messages from people who aren't aware that you're away from your desk, the horror!), but it's perfectly normal to go for walks outside, eat lunch away from your computer, and even take a quick nap break. If you tell your team that you'll be away (either by messaging the group or by setting it as your status), it's signalling to them that it's okay for them to do that too.

This creates a more balanced day, where you can actually get more work done because you're recharging your mental energy. If you need the extra motivation, explicitly schedule time to do this into your workday. There are two benefits to doing this: since it's on your calendar, you're more likely to go for it instead of pushing off breaks until the end of the day (until it's just time to stop working altogether), and you're blocking off that time so that no one else can book meetings or schedule other activities on top of it and throw off your routine. It's a great practice that works for many things—I've seen people schedule dog walks, baby playtime, picking kids up from school, and yoga. I sometimes ride my bike, put on a laundry, or go for a run in the middle of the day to get a boost of energy.

To help create this work/life separation, Trello suggests implementing simple team routines like ending the day by having everyone share the day's highs and lows on Slack, then all ending the workday at the same time together, to really enforce that the day is now over (just like when you see people walking out of the office to go home, when in person).[1]

Time Away from Work

Time away from work is probably the first thing that comes to mind when thinking of ways to recharge. But we also know (at least from my experience working in Canada with a North American culture around work) that it can be difficult to just schedule a whole week or two off (let alone three), *especially* as a manager when you have a lot of people reporting to you, and many responsibilities that require thoughtful planning before being delegated, to avoid throwing anyone into a panic.

---

[1] https://blog.trello.com/help-employees-overcome-burnout

For people in that same situation, while not exactly the same, a highly underutilized tactic to recharge without requiring much (if any) planning is to take half-days off during the week. I find that I recharge the most when I know that others are still working hard while I'm relaxing—which makes it hard for me to fully recharge over periods such as long holiday breaks in December. Taking a Wednesday afternoon or Thursday morning off means that you can get away from work without too much disruption to your schedule since everyone should be able to get by with just a few hours of your absence, and it gives you time to do things you'd normally want to do over the weekend, but without the weekend crowd. It's not a replacement for a true vacation, but when spread out throughout the year, these little breaks can make a big difference in how you approach work and how you go about taking time for yourself.

I should note though that I recognize that not every country or workplace allows for this approach to vacations. Many other countries also provide far more vacation than the typical North American company does, and the culture around that means that people are better at truly disconnecting and taking time for themselves. This is a shortcoming in our own system, but we have to make do.

Talk About It

Talk about how you're doing. It might feel cheesy, but talking about how you're feeling is a big step toward being able to recognize signs of onset burnout before it's too late. If you have peers that you trust at your company and can regularly talk with honestly about how work is going, that's terrific! I find it's also good to talk at a high level about it with your team too. If I have too many meetings and I'm feeling tired out from them, I'll let them know and move a few low-priority meetings to the following week. It creates a space where it's okay for them to be open and honest about how they're doing too, and it will make them more likely to let you know when they're also starting to feel a bit overwhelmed, creating space for changes to be made so that they don't continue down that path.

Takeaways from This Chapter

- Your team members are employees first, not friends or family. Be empathetic and listen and accommodate for what is going on in their lives, but don't overstep boundaries and pry for details or try to problem-solve the issues in their lives outside of what directly results from work. It's not healthy for you, and could be seen as an uncomfortable overstepping of power to them.

- Signs of burnout include a change in communication patterns (frequency of messages, tone, tardiness to meetings, …), a change in work patterns (time of day that work is getting done, overall quality of work, and feelings toward that work), and lowered overall interest in the projects that they're working on.

- There are many things that you can do to try to prevent burnout in you and your team in the first place, including pausing work notifications after the workday is done and scheduling time to do activities away from your screen (walks, lunch, yoga, …).

- Taking half-days throughout the year (on top of your regularly scheduled real vacation) can be a good way to recharge on a continuous basis, without the need to plan for your departure and delegate responsibilities in the same way as you would for longer vacations.

- Talk about how you're doing and your current mental load with trusted peers at work, and possibly even your team. By doing so, you create a space for them to also open up when things are getting to be too much, making room for changes to be made far before any burnout happens, without them feeling guilty about how they're doing.

- If you're going to have a conversation with someone about potential burnout, do it during a regularly scheduled one-on-one so that you don't make it even worse by throwing yet another meeting onto their calendar.

- Burnout can look a lot like underperformance. If someone appears to have the symptoms of burnout, it's possible that they're just bored of what they're working on and need a change.

- When determining whether you're on the path to burnout, pay more attention to the symptoms rather than the behaviors, since you're less likely to notice those in yourself.

CHAPTER 9

Saying Goodbye

The book opened with the initial phases of the employee lifecycle—hiring and onboarding—so it's only natural to bookend it with this last chapter: Saying Goodbye, when people leave the company.

No matter the circumstances, it's an emotional time when someone is leaving: for you as the manager, the person leaving, and the remaining team. Every situation will be different based on the team dynamics and the reason for departure, but there will be some mix of sadness, worry, anger, excitement, and possibly even relief in the air. On a remote team, these feelings are less apparent since you aren't all sitting in a room together all day, and can even tend more toward the general sense of "worry" than you'd see on a colocated team. The most common reaction that I've seen when someone is let go is worry from people that weren't working alongside them daily—because "what if they're next"? It's easy to assume that those you don't work closely with are doing good work, especially remotely where there's little to no exposure or interactions with them compared to when you're sharing an office space. To see them leave the team can come as a surprise and instill the fear that if a seemingly average person was fired, what's stopping them from being next. This is just one part of why having a proper plan for terminating employees and communicating about their departure is so important to the health of remote teams and each individual on them—even those that are leaving.

There are many technical requirements around people leaving, and they vary a lot from company to company. In the same way that we

© Alexandra Sunderland 2022
A. Sunderland, *Remote Engineering Management*,
https://doi.org/10.1007/978-1-4842-8584-8_9

didn't talk about the more administrative tasks in Chapter 2, we won't be covering topics such as how to retrieve someone's company-provided laptop, or managing account access and deactivation. That category of tasks likely belongs to a fully formed set of processes owned by human resources or IT. We don't want to mess with that.

Instead, this chapter is going to be addressing the parts that might result in a more emotional response, like how to best communicate with the person who is leaving in an empathetic way, how to announce it to your team without causing stress and worry, and how to process the departure yourself—because having someone leave the team is hard to deal with, especially when you can't even be physically present for that moment with them. It's hard when someone is leaving by their own volition, or of yours. When it's their choice, it hits hard because it means someone actively decided to remove themselves from your team, and that can feel very personal and painful if it's a surprise (or possibly exciting, in cases where you might have been helping them find a new position where they can grow in their career). It's also hard when it's not their choice, but in a different way: you know that you'll be causing them pain, and we're naturally wired to avoid that and all get along. Even in the most difficult of situations where there may be some strong reason for letting them go independent of their work performance (e.g., inappropriate behavior toward coworkers), the decision and the impact it will have on their life can weight very heavily on your own emotional and mental state.

Employee Termination

We'll start off by talking about what's most likely the more difficult (both logistically and emotionally) and hopefully also far less common scenario: someone on your team is not meeting expectations, and the best course of action is to fire them.

Performance Expectations

Being let go for underperformance should *never* come as a surprise to the affected person. When someone is underperforming and isn't receiving regular direct feedback about the problem, they might not even be aware that there's an issue or that their job is at risk. It's always been important to be in constant communication with team members about their performance, but even more so in cases where a lack of improvement means termination.

Providing that much-needed feedback can be hard for those that are confrontation-averse: it's much easier to say "it's okay, but try to hit the deadline next time" than it is "missing deadlines is an issue because of X, and we need to fix this"—and while it may feel like they understand just how big of a deal repeatedly missing deadlines is, they won't truly internalize it until it's communicated clearly to them. You can't put together a case to let someone go when you haven't even given them the chance to turn things around. Let them know early what needs improving, and give them concrete examples and steps to get better, with frequent updates on how they're progressing. And most of all, in the words of John and Melissa Nightingale, be "Super F*cking Clear."[1] Don't beat around the bush and tell them it would be nice if they were a little faster here and there. Tell them up front that they need to accomplish X, Y, and Z to bring their performance up to standard by a particular date, and if relevant, what any potential consequences might be. Performance management is a key aspect of being a manager, and without providing feedback and setting clear expectations, the team won't necessarily know what "good" work looks like, leading to these types of situations. Not having those two components in place (or setting them up too late) will make the termination conversation even more difficult if they're confused and

---

[1] https://fellow.app/supermanagers/melissa-johnathan-nightingale-raw-signal-group-owning-the-manager-role/

saying that they wished they knew that they weren't meeting expectations beforehand—shifting the blame from themselves to their manager, and making it even more painful to get through for everyone.

Goals and Performance Improvement Plans

When having the conversation with the employee about improving performance, it's helpful to set specific and measurable goals that indicate that they're performing at the expected level. This makes it extremely clear what needs to be done for them to stay in their position, which can eliminate a lot of the uncertainty that a vague "you need to do better work" would bring on.

Some companies implement official ways of doing this, typically called Performance Improvement Plans, or PIPs. These have developed a negative connotation and are sometimes seen as a signal to engineers that a company is only creating a paper trail so that they have an easier time firing you, they've already made their decision, and the outlined goals are so unrealistic to ensure you fail to meet them. If that's not your intention with this (which I truly hope it isn't), it would be a good idea to avoid using that terminology to prevent the person from thinking that's what's happening. There should also be a lot of focus on making it clear that you *do* want them to succeed and continue to be a member of the team. Make sure that these goals are written down and not just communicated verbally, so that they have a way to refer back to them and you can make sure that you're on the same page about what's expected, and there's no room for dispute later on if they aren't met.

These components are necessary to create good goals for these types of plans, based on the SMART acronym:

- **Specific:** Everyone will have a different understanding of what something like "Write more tests" means. But there's no debating what's meant by "Write unit tests for all of the helper methods in your current project." Specific goals pinpoint exactly what is to be done, and leave no room for misinterpretation.

- **Measurable:** This can sometimes be tricky for engineering goals which are often more qualitative than quantitative—but a boolean "has completed"/"has not completed" still counts as measurable! Where possible, be specific with numbers (e.g., "Write 20 unit tests") so that the intent of the goal is clear.

- **Achievable:** Don't set them up for failure by creating an unrealistic goal. The goals should be realistically achievable by the average member of the team who is in good standing.

- **Relevant:** The goal should be related to the type of work that they're already doing.

- **Time-bound:** The date by which the goal should be achieved, as precisely as possible. This might be early on for an incremental goal, or might be the date by which you will be making a decision about whether the person should continue to work at the company. Aim for a specific date instead of vague "by mid-Q2"-type dates which could be misinterpreted. The date should be close enough that they aren't struggling for too long, but far enough away that they have time to make meaningful improvements and demonstrate consistency. Anywhere from 2 weeks (for small startups with just a handful of engineers) to 12 weeks (for large international companies) is a good timeframe, with 6 being a solid starting point.

If you're going through this process with someone and you don't already have weekly one-on-ones, now is the time to implement them. You don't want to just create this plan, hand it over, and see them in three months when they're supposed to have met them and give a pass/fail—that's not helpful to anyone. You need to be getting together regularly and giving feedback on their progress toward meeting those goals to help improve their likelihood of succeeding, and to show that you do in fact care about them.

During this process, you'll also need to be aware that it's possible they've been spooked into thinking they'll be let go, or that they aren't wanted on the team, and they may start to look for another job. This might even be a good thing! If they're going through this plan because they're bored with the work or aren't aligned with the team's vision which is impacting their willingness to perform at the expected level, then it might be in their best interest to move on to a new employer where they can feel more engaged—so this could have a positive effect on their life overall.

Understanding the Underlying Situation

Before setting up any sort of plan or goals, start by questioning why the performance issues that led to being in this situation are happening in the first place. It's easy to blame the lack of progress in a project on an engineer who is coding "too slowly," but that surface-level observation might not be properly explaining what's actually going on. There are many other possible explanations, and a discussion should take place with the person before proposing any kind of plan for improvement.

For example, is it possible that every other engineer on the team is working overtime and artificially getting ahead while this one person is working a normal workweek and perfectly on track for what would be considered normal expectations, but is seemingly behind compared to others? Is it possible that the feature that's taking longer than expected to build is progressing slowly because the product team has been changing their requirements every day for the last few weeks, erasing a lot of the engineer's work each time? Or maybe even, is it possible that they sprinted so hard in the last few months and are starting to get burned out, and could really use more support from the company in recovering properly, instead of being handed a plan to push them even harder? There are many reasons they may be in this situation, so start by focusing on listening to them to get a better understanding of what's going on from their point of view before jumping to any conclusions. They will know a lot more about the current state of their own work than anyone else will, and there might have been things going on behind the scenes that they didn't want to complain about or burden you with.

Often when someone isn't performing well, it's not that they aren't a good employee—it's that they aren't in the right role for their current skillset or interests. An engineer working on infrastructure projects that isn't getting up to speed at the same pace as the others on their team might excel if they're moved to a frontend role focused on interfaces. Even though they're both software engineering disciplines, I would absolutely fail out of an infrastructure-based role in the first week, but could stand my ground (and have) in a product engineering role. There are many, many different types of engineering, all with vastly different skillsets, types of thinking required, and expectations. It's unlikely that someone will be absolutely terrific in all engineering positions, and they just need to find the right one for them and their interests.

Before making a decision to let someone go, and while evaluating their performance, think about whether they're in the right role for what they're good at, and whether they're doing something that interests them. There has already been a lot of effort on both your part and their part to join the company and start to get up to speed, so it may be in both your best interests to find them a different and more suitable team to be a part of so that they can shine.

If at the end of the timeline they've managed to hit the goals, terrific! The rest of this chapter won't be needed. They're now hopefully meeting the standards set out for the team as a whole. Don't stop your efforts with growing them though—employee development is a marathon, but they may have treated this short timeline like a sprint. It's important to continue to meet regularly and evaluate together how they're performing to make sure that they don't slip back into old work patterns.

If however they have *not* been able to meet the agreed-upon goals, then it may be time to have a hard conversation with them. Before making any big decisions, start by considering now that the timeline is over whether those goals were attainable in the first place. If a goal was to complete a particular feature which is still only half done, it might not have been possible no matter what because of a large incident that took over the majority of their time, or they were required on a different high-priority project. The decision should never be a clear go-no-go based *solely* on metrics and a pass/fail on the goal list, and should take into account a more subjective view of the situation. It is however important that that subjectivity still looks at the facts in front of you, and isn't swayed by emotion or the fear of letting someone go—a very real possibility especially when *some* improvement has been made, and you generally get along with them.

Communication As a Vital Skill

One of the hard things about remote work is that you can't just be good at the work: you have to be good at the remote part too.

Someone could be the most terrific programmer in the world and thrive in an office environment where they're surrounded by people and it's easy to tap them on the shoulder when the team is heading over to the conference room for meetings, or to ask for a status update. But that same person could be a terrible colleague in a remote environment, where while their code is of the same caliber, they aren't on top of communicating with their teammates, are consistently late or absent from meetings, and take longer than they should to reply to messages. These behaviors make it impossible for them to work collaboratively in a remote environment, and so in most circumstances make it very difficult for them to be an effective member of the team. Working with people with those behaviors can be extremely frustrating for those alongside them, and can cause people to become so upset that they contemplate leaving the team themselves because no one is doing anything about the problem. It starts to take a toll on the team's mental state and performance as a whole.

It can be difficult to think about how those aspects of communication can be a reason to let someone go from the team when their "real" work is otherwise good, but communication is a vital part of someone's job, too. As we talked about in all the other chapters in this book, communication is the foundation of making a remote environment work. And if someone isn't able to adapt to that and communicate in the expected way after guidance, then remote work might not be right for them—which is okay! It's not for everyone, but it's best to figure this out as soon as possible and remove them from the company if they can't adapt, before it has too much of an effect on others. In the same breath, remote-first communication skills should be assessed in interviews. In Chapter 1, we talked about how you can use a Slack channel for certain portions of the interview process to better understand how they communicate and what it might be like to communicate with them remotely; that's one way of determining whether they'll be a good fit given the expectations of the team.

The Goodbye Conversation

Now comes the hard part. You've decided along with HR and any other critical stakeholders that this person on your team should no longer be employed by the company.

In Chapter 6, we talked about how no one should ever feel forced to turn on their video for meetings, and it's up to each individual to decide for themselves whether to enable their camera unless there are particular circumstances. This is one of those circumstances where you, them, and any other participants should have your video enabled. It allows for them to better understand the situation and absorb what is happening emotionally, and it makes it easier for you to see that they have heard what you're telling them and that they understand, at a time where they may be at a loss for words. And yes, it sucks, especially when remote meetings can be so terrific for hiding feelings, and everyone is now having to display and see the many emotional responses that will happen on this call.

When you're in the meeting, keep it as short and to the point as possible—and don't start with small talk, it will later feel not genuine, and minimizes the importance of the situation. No one, especially the person in question, is going to want to stay on the call for long. If you've gone through all right motions and have worked with them to create a plan for improvement and given them proper feedback along the way as to whether or not they're meeting those expectations, this call will not come as a surprise to them; though that doesn't make it any easier. Stick to the facts, let them know what's going to happen next with their upcoming pay period and how to ship any equipment back to the company, ask if they have any questions, and then thank them for their time and end the call. If you believe in the person and they just weren't the right fit for the needs of the team, you can even offer to write them a letter of recommendation or act as a referral at this point.

A challenge of working remotely in this situation is that you don't have the ability to immediately take away their laptop and walk them out of the building—and also, they're likely taking this call from that same laptop and on their corporate videoconferencing account. In an in-person setting, you'll usually find that the employee accounts get deactivated while they're in the room finding out the news, but the same can't be done here. One of the administrative tasks that HR and IT would be taking care of is to deactivate those accounts immediately after the call has ended. This feels cruel, especially when they might be so far away and their job and means of communication with their teammates have just been taken from them, but this is an emotional time and the company's interests need to be protected. It's good to be aware that this is the case though, and you won't have the opportunity to send a quick message to them after the call. If there are certain things you want to remember to say, create a private note for the call with those talking points to avoid the need for further (sad) communication later.

Announcing Departures

You might already be feeling pretty guilty when you've just fired someone and caused a disruption to their life. But you'll feel it all over again when you announce to the team that they're no longer there too. Don't feel that way! If you did everything we've talked about throughout this chapter, they had ample time and understanding of what to do in order to stay on the team. It's most likely not your fault. The person who was let go will also not be blaming you, but rather be upset with themselves for not being able to meet expectations. The team will also most likely not blame you for letting the person go—but if it was the right thing to do, they might blame you for taking so long to do it.

The most common thing I've heard when someone is let go is a giant common sigh of relief from the rest of the team. Often, if you're noticing performance issues with someone, their teammates are noticing them tenfold. While the performance issues might impact deliverables and timelines that might vaguely get in your way as a manager and cause concern, these things are actively making work life worse for those working directly with them. When people are slow to deliver on code with a shared deadline, the other engineers will pick up the slack and do more than their fair share. When the code quality just isn't where it should be, they'll spend time teaching best practices and rewriting code that they shouldn't have needed to. When there are communication issues and they aren't receiving enough updates to properly work on the project, they'll be throwing their hands in the air and annoyed for having to put up with such issues. They might have even brought up these issues before, which is how the decision was made that there needed to be a change to this person's work habits—but they also might have thought that the issues are all so obvious, and didn't bring them up, or they weren't aware that you knew of the issues and were trying to rectify them. So, often, when that person is no longer on the team, the rest of the team can breathe a little easier knowing that they will be less frustrated with work going forward and things will be a little less hectic. So do not feel guilty when telling your team that someone is no longer there; they might not show it, but if they worked closely with them, it will likely be a load off of their minds.

So how do you go about actually announcing a departure to your team? There are two cases: voluntary and involuntary departures.

Involuntary Departures

In other words, someone has been let go. To best protect the privacy of that person and to avoid unintentionally causing any rumors around their departure, notify the team of the news immediately. This should be done as soon as possible after the termination call: since the employee's accounts will be deactivated, it will be possible for their teammates to find out for themselves if they attempt to reach out to them on the company's messaging platform, or if they notice the total number of people in a channel go down by one, or a meeting invite they send to their email address bounces back.

The best medium for announcing this is over email, where you can't react with emojis (whether good or bad ones), and it's less likely to spark in-thread discussions—since replying to all in an email has a very different feeling than doing the same in an instant messaging platform. Be short and up front that the person has left the team effective immediately, and that you wish them well (if not parting on bad terms—this might be inappropriate in some situations). There is no need to directly say that they were fired, it will be implied by the sudden departure and lack of goodbye on their part. There will likely be questions from people on the team, especially if they weren't working closely with that person—it might appear to be entirely random and unexpected to them, which can cause a bit of fear. You don't owe anyone an explanation of exactly what went wrong and what steps were taken to try to avoid being in this situation; that's private information and shouldn't be divulged. But you can assure people that it was not a surprise, and that you did what was best for both their careers and the team.

Voluntary Departures

In other words, someone has decided that they no longer want to be on your team. Or maybe, they just found another team they would rather be a part of.

This is also a very not-fun situation to be in, but in a different way because the effects that it has on both you and the team are entirely different even though the same concept is applied—someone is leaving the team. This is hard on you because it's very likely out of your control. If you're lucky, the only reason they decided to leave is for higher compensation, and your company is able to match or beat what they were offered, making them perfectly happy and allowing them to stay on your team. But more often than not, if someone has even just *started* to look for a new job, they're already committed to leaving the team; it's difficult to change that since it can be the result of boredom or a values/product mismatch, and you'll need to be prepared for them to go. It's also tough for the team to process because, like you, they're getting the signal that someone no longer wants to work with them (or no longer likes them enough to put up with the work that they're doing there), and that there's a team out there that they see as being better.

It's hard for everyone, even the person who is leaving, who is aware that they're hurting multiple people with the decision and potentially even putting them in a tough position where they'll need to deal with the extra work on top of hiring a backfill for a while—maybe even in a crunch-time period. But people leave jobs all the time, and we get over it all the time.

The way that you go about announcing this type of change is extremely different from the last scenario. The communication around this is often coordinated with the person who is leaving, and it might even be something that *they* want to announce instead of it coming from their manager. They might also want to let a few specific people at the company know before the broader team finds out—for example, if they've been working there for a long time and have become really close with some of their teammates.

There are two best options for announcing this: either at a team meeting or over email. Either way, the communication should involve talking about the great impact that the person has had at the company, when their last day will be, and if there are any changes that will be made to accommodate for it—for example, if they were a manager or team lead, then their role will absolutely need to be figured out before the announcement, even if it's just determining an interim person. If there is an interim person, they must be aware and must have agreed to be in that position ahead of this communication.

When announcing the departure, while it's good to recognize the impact that the person has had on the team and thank them for all of their contributions, don't go so far as to make the rest of the team nervous about how they'll accomplish things without them. For example, if you talk about how critical they are for certain sets of projects, that may worry the others who will start to wonder how they'll get that work done without them, and whether they're going to be put in a bad position and should also start looking for a new job. You do not need to cover why the person is leaving, and no one has to share what they're planning on doing next—though many do choose to, which can help turn the conversations from sadness over a teammate leaving to excitement for their next adventure.

When it's time for them to actually leave on their last day, it can feel very underwhelming and odd to just close a laptop as the marker for the end of a job with a team of people. Assuming you're on good terms, it's nice to close off their employment with a video call between them and the team as a celebration of their time there, the length of which highly depends on team dynamics. Alternatively, the team and any others who worked closely with them can sign an ecard that gets sent to their personal email so that they have a token of appreciation—something that often people will give in physical form in an in-office setting, but is definitely impractical when working remotely.

Offboarding

Just as we talked about in Chapter 2 where strong processes to welcome people into the company are critical, creating good offboarding processes provides a lot of value. This is an important process to have not only for the person leaving but for all of the other team members who will have to cover the gap left by the person until you can hire someone to take over the extra work.

The offboarding process in this case will refer only to what needs to be done when someone is choosing to leave the team. There are two main items for this: knowledge transfer and exit interviews.

Knowledge Transfer

Every person on the team has a certain amount of knowledge that only they know. It might not be critical knowledge, and it might be things that are easy to figure out if you look through the code at least a little bit, but it could also be a highly difficult and critical portion of the project— especially if they've been on the team for a long time and have a lot of knowledge from the years of decisions and mistakes.

Ideally, they'll have been teaching everyone these things and creating documentation as it all comes up. But things happen, and there will always be a handful of topics that never made it into written form. When someone decides to leave, they might decide that they don't want to put the team in a bad position, and will start writing out basically everything that they know so that they could have any possible question answered. But with just two weeks' notice, projects to wrap up, and people checking in to say bye, that takes away a lot of the free time they would have had to write up documentation, and the result is usually a little bit of a sloppy mess that breezes past some critical things and goes far too in depth in others. This isn't the best approach! This is typically a pretty one-sided task, with the departing engineer thinking "only I know X, so I'll write about that." But what should really be happening is asking the remaining team what information they would like to have from that person. Building the list of items that need to be written or talked about needs to be a collaborative effort so that everyone gets the information that they need.

Being a remote team provides the perfect environment for this sort of knowledge transfer. Documentation is great and should be written, but there's rarely time for that in fast-paced environments—and by the time it's written, it needs to be updated. What I find to be truly beneficial for everyone when someone is leaving is to have "brain dump" sessions, where the person will schedule a call with a handful of team members, share their screen, and walk them through the particular thing that they know. This gives the others the chance to ask questions and really understand what's going on while they're still there. The best part is that these sessions can be recorded. They can then serve as training for new hires, and can be rewatched when writing out the documentation for it or trying to work with the code related to that topic. This doesn't come nearly as naturally in in-person offices where you can't usually easily record a meeting and capture all the questions on audio properly. Remote prevails here! Each brain dump session should likely include different people. Everyone will be overloaded if they're sitting in a meeting for eight hours learning everything, and will forget a lot of it by the end of the day. Spread the knowledge around so that each person knows a few more things—but make sure that there are at least two to three people per session. By having these sessions with multiple people, you're reducing the amount of brain dump sessions that would need to happen in the future too: since this single engineer is spreading their knowledge to a few others, when those people leave they won't be the only ones that know that particular thing, and so they won't need to schedule those same sessions again. They will however need to schedule different ones, because this is realistically a problem that will never truly go entirely away.

Exit Interviews

Exit interviews are when you ask the person who is leaving a series of questions. They're not like job interviews, making sure that they know all the things that they were supposed to know. Their purpose is to get honest feedback from the departing employee so that the company can evolve, and possibly even prevent people from leaving in the future for similar reasons.

The idea is that since people are leaving and their career progression will no longer be tied to what the company thinks of them, they'll be more honest than they otherwise would be if they were staying on. In reality, everyone knows not to be completely honest in these interviews. Even if you might not want to work for the same company again, the people who are there will move around to other places too, and you wouldn't want your career or job prospect to be ruined there because of some harsh words you had to say about them at a previous company. "Don't burn bridges" is what you'll hear people say, and so even if you're leaving because of a terrible culture or something is going terribly wrong and somehow the people in charge just aren't noticing it, it won't necessarily be brought up, and they might end up with even more people leaving the team in the near future.

Once one person leaves a team that doesn't have a bright future or is in "Keep the Lights On" mode (no new development), it almost gives "permission" to others on the team to leave as well, and there will be a wave of exits until only a few people are left, who don't leave because of the guilt of totally abandoning a project or the last remaining person. You can't rely on these exit interviews with the HR team to bring out big truths and important insights that will help move the team in a better direction. This is why it's also very important to create a culture of feedback on the team early on, like we talked about in Chapter 7. By creating that culture, filled with retrospectives and surveys where actual change comes about, hopefully the team won't even be in that situation in the first place because all major issues will have been resolved as they happen, and when the exit interview happens, there truly will be nothing large to talk about.

So how can you make the best use of time out of the exit interview? First of all, you should have your own scheduled with the person leaving, separate from the one that they'll be having with human resources. You know your team's work much more intimately than any other person in the company would, and so you're able to ask the most pointed questions and pull out the greatest insights—it's worth the time to go over it all. These calls should be scheduled for about an hour, and take place in the last two to three days of their time at the company. Don't wait until the very last day to schedule it, they'll be very busy wrapping other things up and trying to leave on a high note; you don't want to drag them down with a hard conversation about feedback.

Before the call, think about what types of things you're going to want to talk about and what aspects of the team you want their opinion on in particular—then write those questions down in a meeting note that they get access to ahead of time. You'll get the best answers if they're able to think about things ahead of time and prepare. It's good to ask pointed and specific questions related to the processes and happenings on your team (like "how did you feel about the company when X happened"), but you can also throw in some more generic questions around why they decided to start looking for something new in the first place, what they most enjoyed about their time here, if they felt heard and equipped to do their job, and if there's anything that if done sooner would have influenced them to stay with the company longer. Set aside time for them to talk about anything that they might want to bring up too; it's possible that there's something they'd like to get off their chest before leaving—perhaps an incident that you should be aware of, or a bad working environment that they didn't feel safe mentioning before. They might also want time to just reminisce with you and talk about all the ways in which the team has changed since they joined. You can also ask for feedback on yourself as a manager, though it's less likely that they'll be candid here since it's still hard to give constructive feedback face to face with someone, and they might leave that portion for when they talk with human resources. But if you do get some insights out of that line of questions, it can be extremely valuable as you can dig deeper and ask follow-up questions to truly understand how you can improve.

Takeaways from This Chapter

- It should never come as a surprise to someone that they're being let go for underperformance. If they aren't meeting expectations, it's your duty as their manager to create goals and timelines that they need to meet, with a clear understanding that they aren't meeting the standards.

- Once you've created a plan with goals and a timeline to be met by an underperforming employee, make sure that you have regular one-on-ones where you're communicating feedback on their progress toward those goals so they aren't left in the dark till they get a pass/fail at the end. This also helps to show that you do care about their improvement, and this isn't just a ruse to create a paper trail to fire them.

- Employee development is a marathon, not a sprint. Make sure that they're continuing their newly formed performance expectations past the timeline set out too.

- Before creating a plan for improvement, talk to the person to understand what might be going on from their point of view. It's very possible that there's something going on behind the scenes that you aren't aware of and is impacting their performance in a way that they can't control. Don't jump to conclusions and blame them for it. You want to be as supportive as possible while starting off this conversation.

- Email the team as soon as possible after someone has been fired so that they find out through you and not by noticing a deactivated account. Do not provide details or explicitly say that they were let go; you owe the person their privacy, and the team will read between the lines since there was no goodbye or heads-up.

- Often, if you're noticing performance issues with someone, their teammates are noticing them tenfold. Don't feel guilty for announcing a departure; it may cause a collective sigh of relief.

- When someone is leaving the team of their own volition, work with them to figure out how they'd like to communicate it. If they've been on the team for a long time, there may be some people they'd like to tell personally before it's announced at the larger scale.

- If you're on good terms when someone is leaving the company, have a goodbye video call for the team or sign a virtual ecard as a nice way to bookend the working relationship instead of marking the end of the era by just them closing their laptop lid one last time.

- Knowledge transfer sessions are very valuable meetings where the engineer who is leaving goes over what they know with a few others on the team. These sessions should be recorded so that they can act as training material for new hires, and can be rewatched when writing documentation to better cover these things that should have been documented before.

- When someone is leaving, they shouldn't spend all their time writing documentation, and shouldn't focus only on the things that they think are important. The input of the people who are staying on the team should be taken into account too so they're learning the things that they know they will need when they're gone.

- Exit interviews should be scheduled for two to three days before their last day, and are a great time to ask questions to surface feedback about how the team works together, and what could make things better overall. They may not be entirely candid to avoid burning bridges, but if done right this can be a great source of information. You'll get the most useful insights out of this meeting if you've already created a culture of feedback on the team.

Index

W, X, Y, Z

Printed in the United States
by Baker & Taylor Publisher Services